The Heart of
EMPATHY

Robert R. Carkhuff, Ph.D.
Bernard G. Berenson, Ph.D.
Jeannette Tamagini, Ed.D.

Published by: HRD Press, Inc.
             22 Amherst Road
             Amherst, Massachusetts 01002
             800-822-2801 (U.S. and Canada)
             413-253-3488
             413-253-3490 (fax)
             http://www.possibilitiesschools.com

ISBN: 978-1-59996-164-4

Editorial services by Robert W. Carkhuff
Production services by Jean Miller and Anctil Virtual Office
Cover design by Eileen Klockars

Table of Contents

About the Authors

In the late 1960s, when individuals for the first time in our country were engaged in a "personal" revolution, **Robert R. Carkhuff** wrote his two-volume classic called *Helping and Human Relations.* In so doing, he opened the doors for the first time to the true definitions of human relating. He hit a nerve. Soon thereafter, *The Art of Helping,* which he carefully designed for the helping professions/ teachers/preachers/therapists and parents, sold more than one million copies. For the first time ever, he researched and defined the outcomes of helping and human relating. These texts soon stood among the most-referenced Social Science works of the twentieth century. Now with his partners, **Bernard G. Berenson** and **Jeannette Tamagini,** Carkhuff returns to reflect upon the values and require-ments of what it takes to be a helper in the twenty-first century.

Carkhuff, a scientist, is Chairman of the Carkhuff Group of Corporations and its flagship, **Human Technology, Inc.** He is responsible for generating major human movements:

- **Human Relations** with *Helping and Human Rela-tions* in 1969
- **Human Resources** with *The Development of Human Resources* in 1971
- **Human Potential** with *Toward Actualizing Human Potential* in 1981
- **Human Productivity** with *Sources of Human Pro-ductivity* in 1983

- **Human Processing** with *Human Processing and Human Productivity* in 1986
- **Human Capital** with *The Age of the New Capitalism* in 1988
- **Human Possibilities** with *Human Possibilities— Human Capital in the 21st Century* in 2000

Berenson is a teacher, lifelong social scientist, and Director of **Carkhuff Institute of Human Technology and Possibilities Science.** Together with Carkhuff, he has introduced twenty-first century civilization to a new body of science dedicated to freedom:

- *The New Science of Possibilities* (2000)
- *The Possibilities Leader* (2000)
- *The Possibilities Organization* (2000)
- *The Possibilities Mind* (2001)
- *The Possibilities Economy* (2005)
- *The Science of Freedom* (2007)
- *The Age of Ideation* (2007)

Tamagini is Professor Emeritus, Rhode Island College, and a contributing author to counseling as a source of freedom:

- *The Art of Helping,* Volumes I–VIII
- *The Freedom Doctrine*

Together, these authors combine decades of study and progress on the subject of human behavior and development into a universal body of work that should be required reading for every individual.

Foreword
The Heart of Empathy

With a lifetime of research, development, and practice, we have studied the effective ingredients of helping and human relations. In the chapters that follow, we will spell out these effects and their sources:

1. **Empathy—The "In-Feeling"**

   Every human interaction from birth to death may have growthful or deteriorative effects upon people, and empathy is the primary source.

2. **Crises in Helping and Life**

   The effects are dependent upon the helpees' ability to manage the crises in their lives or to find helpers who can.

3. **The Facilitators**

   The **Facilitators** are helpers who facilitate the helpees' movement through the processes of helping—exploring, understanding, acting.

4. **The Retarders**

   The **Retarders** "pretend" to be helpers who retard the helpees' movement through helping processes.

5. **Facilitators and Retarders**
   - The **Facilitators** are **"Light-Side"** helpers who are accurately responsive and operationally initiative.
   - The **Retarders** are **"Dark-Side"** people who are insensitively initiative and noninitiatively responsive.

6. **Research and Development**
   - R & D on empathy shapes the development of the helping skills technology.
   - Research culminates in 96 percent positive outcomes in more than one hundred thousand living, learning, and working cases.

7. **On Becoming Empathic**

   One of the things that makes us truly human is our ability to relate. **True Facilitators** relate as follows:
   - Responding to **GET** others' images
   - Initiating to **GIVE** our own images
   - Negotiating to **MERGE** our new image

8. **The Heart of Empathy**
   - Empathy is the ultimate expression of freedom for both helper and helpee.
   - Empathy is the **"sacred trust"** because it empowers us to leave people better than we found them.

RRC   January 2009
BGB   McLean, VA
JT

1

Empathy—
The "In-Feeling"

The term **"empathy"** is derived from the German word **"einfuhling,"** meaning the **"in-feeling"** where one person has the **"equivalent"** of another person's experience. In modern times, empathy is defined generically as **"the capacity for participating in and understanding the feelings or ideas of another."**

These simple definitions have profound significance in human terms:

- Most people have never had an empathic experience with another. To this depressing experience, we may respond empathically:

  "You feel hopeless because you have never managed to connect your humanity with another's."

- Some people have felt empathic experiences with others but have been unable to communicate them. To this frustrating experience, we may also respond empathically:

  "You feel so unfulfilled because you are cheated of the rewards of communicating."

- Some few people have had empathic experiences and have been able to share fully with others. To this elevating experience, we may now respond empathically:

  "You feel so elated because you have become 'one' with another person."

We may view the instance of empathy most clearly in the good mother's relationship with her child. She positions herself for **"hovering attentiveness"** to her child's appearance and behavior. She communicates a **"penetrating understanding"** of her child's experience—both verbally and nonverbally. She is, in short, an extension of the child, just as the child is for her.

At this point, we may stop the video and share with the good mother **our penetrating understanding of her experience:**

> **"You feel ecstatic because you are 'one' with your child."**

Clearly, the empathic experience of **"penetrating understanding"** is not restricted to genetically feminine type. Some of us have known men who experienced this understanding in **"virtually nursing"** their children. There are many other illustrations of this **"penetrating understanding"** as we shall soon find, for empathy pervades all areas of human relating.

It is precisely this **"penetrating understanding"** that is the subject of empathy—not simply **"to walk in others' shoes,"** but to experience the world as others do. In effect, to become "one" with the other person:

> **"You feel whole because you are now 'one' with others."**

That is the feeling of **"empathy":** to become **"one"** with another and his or her images or ideas about the world.

In healthy people and families, empathy is the lifelong **"connectivity"** with the diversity and changeability of human experience. This **"connectivity"** is found in the evolving experience of a young person's poem:

ROLLING
On Being Alive

I am rolling, rolling, rolling
I see the earth
I see the sky
I am rolling, rolling, rolling

When I was three
I loved the earth and sky
I loved others and myself
As only innocence could love.

When I was six
I loved the earth and sky
I loved others and myself
As others love to love.

When I was twelve
I liked the earth and sky
I loved others and myself
As others love to love.

When I was twelve
I liked the earth and sky
I liked others and myself
Sometimes!—and under certain circumstances.

When I was twenty-four
I could no longer love the earth and sky
I could no longer love others or myself
I could no longer love at all.

Then a child, however old
Took me by the hand and said,
"See the earth, See the sky"
And through his eyes I saw again.

Finally, I am me once more
I love the earth and sky
I love the others as myself
As only the courageous can love.

I am rolling, rolling, rolling
I see the earth
I see the sky
I am rolling, rolling, rolling.

The Origins

The origin of empathy is the love of self and its extensions in life. We may view this love in the secure child who embraces all people and all experiences she/he encounters. We often wonder at the explosiveness of the child's love. Yet it is we, the adults, who have given her the intensity of love and security that is a precondition for empathy.

Because of the **"empty spaces"** in the experiences of the undernourished and insecure person, she/he can never experience **"equivalency"** of feeling with another person or phenomenon. At best, she/he can subtract from the experiences of the other; at worst, she/he can distort the experiences so that the other cannot build upon them.

Sympathy vs. Empathy

First of all, empathy is not to be confused with sympathy. Empathy is **"other-centered"** or other-directed and embraces the full range of human experiences—from happiness to sadness or depression:

> **"You feel strong because you can now discriminate between empathy and sympathy."**

Sympathy, in turn, is **"speaker-centered"** or inner-directed and emphasizes the ancient Greek interpretation of **"sharing the suffering of another"**:

> **"I feel your pain!"**

Once again, the empathic response facilitates wide-ranging exploration of experience. In turn, sympathy is more like an official pronouncement or diagnosis of a painful or even terminal condition. It often borders on **"schadenfreude"** or **"joy in the suffering of others."** In short, empathy opens things up while sympathy closes them down.

In this context, the use of the adjective **"empathetic"** usually reflects the person's confusion over being empathic and/or sympathetic:

> **"You feel conflicted because you don't know whether to concentrate upon the feeling it evokes in you or the feeling of the other person."**

The simple truth is that people who are only partially formed cannot be empathic or **"equivalent"** with people or phenomena that are struggling to be fully formed.

Sources of Empathy

The sources of empathy are the sources of all learning (see Table 1-1): generating, modeling, experiential, didactic, reinforcement. As may be noted, parents and their surrogates are the original sources of this learning, and children, in their evolving development, are the recipients. We can study the effects of learning empathy with five levels of paradigms.

Generating is the most powerful paradigm for learning anything. At the highest levels of generating, people participate empathically in interdependent processing: **mutual relating for mutual processing.** To contribute to the genesis of an experience or an idea is the pre-potent source of all learning.

Modeling is the second most powerful paradigm for learning empathy. Healthy parents present learnable behaviors of empathy in their loving marriages and families and extended families. Children learn to imitate these behaviors and, however much they may deviate from them in their lives, tend to return to the basic models set for them in home and family.

Table 1-1.
Primary Sources of Empathy

Paradigms	Sources	Recipients	Effects
5. Generating	Creators	Contributors	Empowerment
4. Modeling	Parents	Children	Imitation
3. Experiential	Helpers	Helpees	Exploration
2. Didactic	Teachers	Learners	Achievement
1. Reinforcement	Authorities	Performers	Performance

Experiential empathy is the third most powerful paradigm for learning empathy. The child or helpee experiences the sensitive understanding of a more mature helper on her/his journey through life. The net effect of experiencing empathy is for the helpees to explore themselves in relation to their worlds.

The fourth most powerful paradigm for learning empathy is the didactic. Here the teacher or authority communicates the principles of empathy in a teaching model. For example, the teacher may communicate **"The Principle of Reciprocal Affect"—people tend to relate to us the way we relate to them.** The net effect is that learners work harder and achieve more for teachers who employ this principle.

Finally, reinforcement is the last most powerful source of learning empathy. In this paradigm, authority figures influence performers throughout their lives by differentially reinforcing them: positively for positive performance; neutrally for neutral performance; punitively for negative performance. Again, the great caveat on reinforcement is the principle of reciprocity: **"Kids don't perform for people they don't like!"**

These sources of empathy learning are integrated in people we label as **"The Facilitators"**:

- **Generating** to experience the **"creation moment"**
- **Modeling** to provide **"hovering attentiveness"**
- **Experiential** to offer **"penetrating understanding"**
- **Didactic** to consolidate **"empathic understanding"**
- **Reinforcement** to sustain **"empathic performance"**

"The Facilitators" demonstrate empathy by concentrating on modeling and experiential learning. They consolidate and sustain the learning with didactic and reinforcement sources. For example, they check in with all important people in their lives by responding to their frames of reference to elicit input for every human endeavor.

In general, however, many people tend to employ learning paradigms in the reverse order of their power. That is why we label them **"Retarders."**

- **Reinforcement** is over-used, especially by people who have not become **"potent reinforcers"** for the recipients.
- **Didactic teaching** is a reflex response for many authority figures who figure that **what they know**— and not **how they communicate**—is most important to teach.
- **Experiential** is little used because it requires the diligent effort of **"hovering attentiveness"** and **"penetrating understanding."**
- **Modeling** remains their least-used paradigm for empathy learning because most people say, **"Do as I say—not as I do!"**
- **Generating** is unavailable to most people because it requires enormous effort in conquering substance.

Relatedly, empathy and its sources of learning are inversely related to authoritarianism. Simply speaking, authoritarians do not relate to another's frame of reference. Put another way, authoritarians cannot afford to relate on their way to their **"preconceived destinations."** Accordingly, command-and-control and other restricting systems employ reinforcement—especially punishment—as their preferred modes of controlling others, usually with few didactic principles to guide them.

The Skills of Empathy

In the final analysis, it is the special skills we have that empower us to become special people or **"helpers."** What are these special skills?

Discrimination and communication are two sets of scientifically validated skills. Communication builds upon discrimination in a developmental manner. This holds true for all would-be helpers with the exception of one population: those who use their discriminations of others' experiences to manipulate them—to get them to say **"Yes,"** to buy the product, to cast the vote. With the exception of this diagnosable pathology (psychopathic), all other healthy people build helpful responses developmentally, from discrimination to communication.

Now let us refer to Table 1-2 to view a simple outline of **"The Skills of Empathy."** As may be noted, five levels are represented, ranging from responding through personalizing to initiating. For each level, discrimination and communication skills are illustrated.

Table 1-2.
The Skills of Empathy

Levels	Discriminations	Communications
1. Responding to Content	**What** is being said?	"You're saying _____."
2. Responding to Feeling	**How** does this make him (her) feel?	"You feel _____."
3. Responding to Meaning	**Why** is he (she) feeling this way?	"You feel _____ because _____."
4. Personalizing Feeling and Meaning	**Who** is responsible for this?	"You feel _____ because you cannot _____."
5. Individualizing New Feeling and Meaning	**Where** does he (she) want to go with this?	"You feel _____ because you can _____."

So for Level 1, we simply repeat the gist of **What** the other person is saying:

"You're saying that things are going well."

At Level 2, we answer the question, **How** this makes the person feel:

"You feel happy."

At Level 3, we answer the question, **Why** the person feels this way:

"You feel happy because things are going well."

At Level 4, we answer the question, **Who** is responsible for this:

> **"You feel disappointed because you're not carrying your part of the load."**

At Level 5, we answer the question, **Where** do you want to go from here:

> **"You feel excited about learning to do your part."**

In these simple illustrations, we have learned the discrimination and communication skills ranging from simple responding to personalizing and individualizing initiatives.

At this point, we may pause to ask the basic question of all human encounters: Are they **"for better or for worse"?**

When we ask this question of audiences, we find astounding results. For example, we remind them that most people have had 100 or so teachers over the course of their lives. Then we ask the basic question:

> **"How many of your teachers related to your frames of reference and empowered you to do things that you had never dreamed yourself capable of?"**

A show of hands reveals that only a smattering of students have had this positive experience: few more than three, rarely any for the marginal students!

To those few people, we respond empathically:

> **"You feel blessed because you were given the opportunity to fulfill your potential."**

Next, we have asked the following question:

> **"How many of your teachers ignored you and actually held you back from doing things that you knew you were capable of doing?"**

Now comes a real show of hands. Almost everyone has had five or more negative experiences. **All** of the minorities had more than five—those that they could remember, that is.

To these people, we respond empathically:

> **"You feel so angry because you were cheated of the opportunity to fulfill your potential."**

If you reflect upon your own schooling, you may come to similar conclusions. Perhaps you, too, have had more retarding than facilitative experiences. Indeed, we may make a good case for defining your degree of **"marginality"** by the lack of responsiveness to your experience:

> **Marginality is the sum-total of experiences devoid of human relating.**

Perhaps the greatest tragedy is that you can't remember the names or even the faces of 90 or so teachers who just did not make a difference!

To those who have had this experience, we respond by personalizing our empathy:

> **"You feel disappointed because you could never reach these sources of nourishment."**

2

Crises in Helping and Life

The pattern of helping, as of life, comprises a series of interrelated crises. We benefit or not as we act constructively or not. Put another way, each crisis encapsulates a process leading to constructive change. In a very real sense, the rest of helping and, indeed, the rest of life is, at best, supportive and, at worst, irrelevant or even destructive.

In order to study the effects of the manipulation of facilitative conditions, what were, in effect, "crises" were experimentally introduced; that is, during the first third of helping, high levels of empathic relating were offered the helpee by the helper. During the second third, relating was lowered when the helper selectively withheld the best possible responses that he might otherwise have made. Here the helper's responses tended to be innocuous rather than precipitously lowered. Finally, during the last period, the conditions were raised again to a highly facilitative level. The sessions were taped and rated. The helpee, then, received low levels of facilitative conditions during the middle period; he was not understood with any degree of sensitivity. The helper's regard and hovering attentiveness were not available to him and the helper was, to some degree, not genuine. In effect, the helpee experienced a relating crisis in the sense that he was attempting to communicate himself but did not receive in return facilitative communications from the helper.

The findings are striking. The depth of self-exploration engaged in by both psychotic people and low-level-functioning students was found to be a direct function of the level of conditions offered by the helper; that is, when the helper offered high levels of empathy, the low-functioning helpees explored themselves at relatively high levels and when the helper offered low levels of empathy, the low-functioning helpees explored themselves at very low levels.

The following excerpts are drawn from the three periods of one of the studies of the experimental manipulation of facilitative conditions. During Period 1, a highly resistant young female helpee functioning at low levels comes gradually to explore herself through the strenuous efforts of her high-level-functioning helper. Note how the helper perseveres in responding to the helpee's anxiety in entering helping.

Period 1

Helper: You keep staring at the tape recorder. You're anxious about getting involved.

Helpee: No, it's the only thing to look at in here.

Helper: You want to avoid my eyes.

Helpee: No, that's not it. I bought a tape recorder two years ago. (Pause) I can't think of anything else to say.

Helper: You just want to escape.

Helpee: I just wish I could think of something to say.

Helper: It's really hard to get started.

Helpee: It never is. I guess I can't help the way I am. But I'd like to change some of my ways.

The helper goes on to become more and more involved in process movement. However, during the experimental second period, this movement ceases, and the exchange, which was dependent on the helper's level of empathic functioning, deteriorates to a level of everyday **"schmoozing"**:

Period 2

Helper: I guess we're both kind of tired.

Helpee: I've been keeping late hours, working weekends, not getting any sleep. I have to rest to catch up on my studies.

Helper: Studies are hard.

Helpee: Yeah, but I like them, too, only not too much.

Helper: Too much is too much.

Helpee: Yeah, sometimes I just get tired, not enough sleep, I guess.

The process is an almost circular one that leads nowhere. It must be reiterated that the helper's responses during the middle period were not negative or destructive in nature but rather reflected the selective withholding of the best possible responses. During the final period, the helper again provides high levels of conditions and the client comes to explore herself at a very deep level.

Period 3

Helper: What you have hidden from the world is pretty precious to you.

Helpee: The world could care less.

Helper: You feel angry because they don't really give a damn.

Helpee: I can't help feeling this way, because they always leave me out.

Helper: You feel disappointed because they're all wrapped up in themselves. Even if you did open up . . .

Helpee: They wouldn't hear me or see me because they don't care. (Sob) So I guess I hide the real me from them.

Thus the helpee proceeds to invest herself further in working out her identity, particularly in relation to others. With the helper tuned in, she makes amazing strides of progress. With the helper functioning at low levels, she cannot take a baby step.

We may view the helper levels of relating and helpee levels of exploring in helper-introduced crises in Figure 2-1. As may be noted, the high-functioning helpee **(He (Hi))** is impacted minimally and returns fluidly to high levels of exploration. In turn, the low-functioning helpee **(He (Lo))** is impacted powerfully and never again returns to moderate levels of exploration. This is the profile for helpers and helpees in helping and in life.

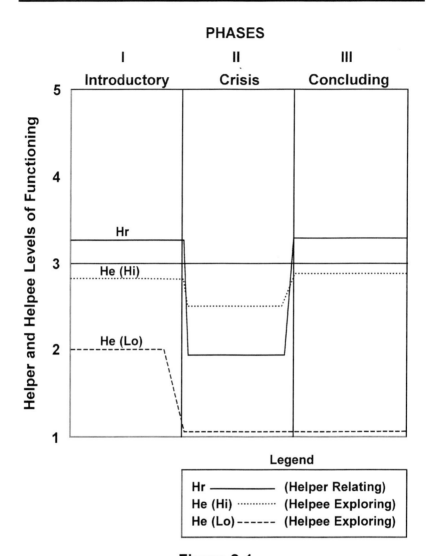

PHASES

Figure 2-1.
Helper Levels of Relating and
Helpee Levels of Exploring in Crises

The Crisis

To summarize, when the crisis involving low levels of communication is precipitated with low-level-functioning helpees, the communication process breaks down totally; the helpee collapses unless there is a facilitative person around to put the communication process together again. On the other hand, when high-level-functioning helpees are seen by high-level-functioning helpers, the crises have less disastrous consequences. Thus, during the middle experimental period, the high-level-functioning helpees continue to explore themselves independently of the helpers' lowering of empathic conditions.

It seems that, once the high-level-functioning helpee is aware that the helper is tuned in on his/her wavelength and genuinely concerned for his/her welfare, he/she continues to function independently of the level of helper-offered empathic conditions. Following the initial period of high-level conditions, the higher the level of helpee functioning, the greater his or her independence of the high-level-functioning helper's conditions.

Life and Death Crises

The physical prototype for the life-and-death crises in relating is the birth experience, where the movement toward life involves the risk of death. Similarly in helping, the helpee seeks his or her fuller emergence or re-emergence, or life, at the risk of death. This can be most clearly seen during early encounters with relatively pathological helpees where in very direct or very subtle ways, the helpee attempts to undermine the helper and the power implicit in his or her role. In a very real sense, although the helpee is drawn to helping, he finds himself quickly attempting to **"take the measure"** of the person sitting across from him. The issue, like all issues in the lives of many helpers, is one of destroying or being destroyed, of incorporating or being incorporated. Thus, in the following example, a young man in his 20s functioning at low levels is confronted by the helper with his engagement in a number of destructive activities. The helpee directly and explicitly describes his motives and intentions:

Helper: John, you are furious and you really want to destroy our relationship here.

Helpee: It's more than that.

Helper: You want to kill me.

Helpee: No, not really. I . . .

Helper: John, you want to kill me.

Helpee: Yes, I want to kill you. I know you haven't earned it, but I want to kill you, maybe for everyone I hate.

Helper: That's too easy. You can't.

Helpee: I can! I can! One way or another I will. So I can't take you this way, but I'll find another. I'll fail you. I'll lead you astray. You'll think I'm improving but I'll fail. I'll be your failure case. You'll be responsible.

Helper: You're committed to do anything you have to, to undermine me, to destroy me, even something that hurts you.

Helpee: Yes. Yes.

Helper: If you can in some way defeat me, you won't have to change your way of living. You do stupid things to protect a stupid way of living, and that's stupid.

Helpee: Oh, I want to change. I do. I can't help it. I can't help it. God, I've been wrong to hurt you.

Helper: You feel relieved of this burden of hatred, but you had to find out whether you could take me. If you could, I couldn't help you, and I can.

It is almost as if the helpee, in his attack, is saying "over-whelm me and give me hope." The helper responds firmly to the helpee's desperate attempts to threaten the helper and to defend his way of living, but, most importantly, he responds to the helpee's deepest need to lose in this encounter and to win in his life. He confronts the helpee with what the helpee is doing but reassures him that there is hope.

Having been unable to overwhelm the helper, the helpee is now confronted with a deeper, even more disturbing motive: that of wanting to give himself fully to this strong person. His dependency needs threaten him even more than his destructive impulse. It is as if he is saying "How can I trust that you will not abuse me if I commit myself to you?" Thus, in a later session, the issue of being incorporated arises.

Helper: You're really saying you don't know if you can trust me.

Helpee: Why should I? How do I know you're not really a neurotic? How do I know that I won't tap in on your need for power or something like that?

Helper: Will I do what you would do in the same circumstances?

Helpee: Will you destroy like I would?

Helper: You're scared of finding out that I am the guy who can help you make it.

Helpee: Can you help me change?

Helper: You've been led down a lot of primrose paths before. That's all over now, though. You've got to know this time.

Helpee: There's no more time. I'm running out of it.

Helper: It's pretty terrifying. This is your only hope . . .

Helpee: But I don't know if I can make the commitment.

Helper: You've got to ask that question—at the deepest level. I'd be worried if you didn't. Your life is at stake.

Helpee: If I commit myself, can I make it? Will you help me?

The question of trust comes up over and over again at deeper and deeper levels of helping. Many helpers are misled by a **"once-over-lightly"** on trust and confidentiality. The helpee's real question is whether he can trust the helper with his life. He asks, "If I can upset him, intimidate him, and destroy him, I cannot trust him. If I cannot destroy him, will he destroy me?"

At another level, the helpee is asking if he can trust himself with his own life. Because the helper sees the helpee's world better than the helpee and enables the helpee to understand his or her world better (goals), the helpee is faced with the first real choice: live or die. Up to the point the helper defines a helping goal and the means to achieve it, the helpee experiences only the choice to die.

Distance and Experience

Throughout the early phases of relating, the issues of all phases of the helpee's experiences come up over and over again at deeper and deeper levels. The helpee who has had a meaningful helping experience may come to doubt the experience after a lapse of time. It is as if the helper's acknowledgment of the experience and its full implications would commit the helpee to further investments of himself without knowing the implications. Each step along the way commits the person to further steps, and the direction cannot always be anticipated. In the following example, the helpee, a woman in her 30s functioning at low levels, had a deeply meaningful experience with the helper at a moment of terror in her life. This was a moment in which she did not know if she could live or would die, a moment in which the helper held out his hand to hold hers through the crisis. During the next encounter, the helpee questions the meaning of the previous encounter:

Helpee: You paw me just like all of the rest. You're just like the rest, you just want something from me.

Helper: You question the whole experience and all of my motives.

Helpee: You want the same thing they want—me.

Helper: You don't trust that it happened.

Helpee: It couldn't have happened.

Helper: There are implications either way.

Helpee: What do you mean?

Helper: If it didn't happen, then you can't trust all of this as real, and you don't have to commit yourself. If it did, well . . .

Helpee: If it happened, it's the first time that anyone ever cared for me, without wanting something in return.

Helper: You feel insecure because you have never been here before.

Helpee: It's sure different and I'm different.

Helper: You've changed, but you're not sure how.

Helpee: I've changed, yet I haven't. I'm still me but I can, I can—begin to see who you are . . . maybe.

Helper: You feel stronger because you have room for someone else now and you have always wanted to.

Helpee: That's it, I've never really left room for others. It's always been just me—and what *they* want.

Helper: You are larger and stronger and want to keep it that way.

The helpee wants to believe but has to doubt. If the previous experience were illusory, it cannot be made real. If the previous experience were real, the helper cannot allow the helpee's analyses to make it illusory. The neurotic's ambition is to make the real illusory and the illusory real. The helper must be deeply in the encounter or he cannot later trust his experience of the encounter any more than the helpee's later expression of his or her experience. Only if the helpee is not allowed to destroy what must live can he enter and trust later life experiences. In addition, the helpee may have a tendency to deny growth because with it comes more work, re-evaluation, and responsibility—the very things the helpee has avoided.

The Honest Confrontation

Throughout each of these examples, the helper has in the end relied on his or her experience of the helpee. At the crisis point, the helper must rely on his experience with helpees functioning below a minimally facilitative, self-sustaining level. Usually at this point, the helper's most effective mode of functioning may involve an honest confrontation with the helpee. This is often because of the time limitations that an unresolved crisis places on therapy.

Although an honest experience with a constructive person is precisely what has been missing in the low-level functioning person's life and is exactly what brings him to helping, he will often do everything possible to prevent its occurrence. He prefers his fantasies to reality. Even for low-functioning helpees, acting and doing cannot compete with insight and talking. The destroyer of his illusions is his murderer. He holds the helper off with intimidation, threatening to make the helper fully responsible for anything deleterious that happens to him. He defines an honest confrontation as a "hostile act." Indeed, any action by anyone is an attack. *Life is death, and death is life.*

If the helper does not acknowledge the crisis, confront it, and in so doing confront the helpee and himself, the helper's passivity reinforces the helpee's passivity. The only real change that might then take place is in the modification of the helpee's perception and the expression of his crises. The consequent insight gives him the feeling or illusion that he is on top of his situation when in reality (and he finds this out when he returns to real life) he is not. He cannot act just as his helper could not act; a real helper is only acting in an honest encounter involving himself and the helpee. Providing high levels of facilitative conditions does not in itself constitute an act but rather, if effective, only increases the probability for action on the part of both helper and helpee. The crises help precipitate honest confrontation between helper and helpee. Traditional forms of helping often neither recognize the crises nor acknowledge the necessity for confrontation for constructive purposes.

A whole helper brings his whole person and all of his accumulated store of knowledge to bear at the crisis point. His very acknowledgment of the crisis dictates his full employment of himself. If the helper is able to "touch" the helpee, letting him know that he is with him in his deepest moment and that he will do whatever he has to do to free the helpee to choose life, then the closed cycle that disallows action is broken. Instead there is an opening movement toward emergence that will, in turn, involve other crises in life. Again, *life is a process of interrelated crises and challenges that we confront to live.*

Confrontation is never necessary, and it is never sufficient! Confrontation within the context of high levels of responding by a whole helper may be efficient. In the following example, the helper precipitates a crisis:

Helper: We've spent several sessions together and I think I have some feeling for who you are.

Helpee: I've really appreciated your understanding. You have been very helpful.

Helper: Not exactly. Are you familiar with the details of the referral?

Helpee: Well, I didn't get along with Dr. S---, and I guess I still have problems with other people.

Helper: JoAnne, you were labeled a psychopath. Do you understand what that means?

Helpee: I guess so, like criminal or something.

Helper: Sort of. For you it means the way you manipulate everyone without concern for their welfare.

Helpee: I guess that's what I did with Dr. S---.

Helper: . . . and others . . . and it's what you'd like to do with me.

Helpee: (Begins to cry.)

Helper: But I am different.

Helpee: I can't believe that I matter that much to you. I know you're different, but I can't help acting that way. I can't help it. I can't help it. (Cries fully.)

Helper: You feel good—in one piece because you really make a difference to me.

Helpee: I don't think anyone ever felt I was important.

Helper: You were angry because you could not make people like you—respect you, but you want to make them respect you.

Now the helpee can choose a new and relevant goal with someone who can help her achieve it. The helpee is on the way to accepting some real measure of responsibility. The helper created the crisis and provided the means to resolve it. The helper, in his living embodiment as well as in his words, confronts her with her choice to destroy others as well as herself. In so doing, he holds out his hand to offer her a chance to choose life.

Traditionally, confrontation has been employed only with delinquent or psychopathic helpees. It seems as if only this population gives the helper license to return the "hostile act." In the following example, a young man functioning at low levels threatens one last potent act, suicide, and the helper responds:

Helpee: . . . you've pushed me too far, that's why.

Helper: You're really saying that if you die, I'm the murderer.

Helpee: You'll have my blood on your hands for everyone to see.

Helper: You've been pushed so hard that you've reached a point where it seems the only thing you can do.

Helpee: That's all.

Helper: That's honest.

Helpee: (After a pause): What do you mean?

Helper: Well, it's either that or choosing to act to live.

Helpee: (After a pause): I've had everything taken from me—all my dreams—I'm back at the beginning, with nothing.

Helper: You're alone but not lost. I am with you. Either way you act, it's got to be for you—just you.

If the helper is indeed guilty, he cannot confront the helpee at this crisis point. The helpee's crisis becomes his, and if he cannot acknowledge the crisis for himself as well as the helpee, constructive change for either cannot ensue. Of course the helper must, as we have emphasized throughout, do more than confront the helpee. He must be willing to accompany the helpee into the deepest, unexplored caverns of the helpee's behavior. The helper is the guide: it is his or her willingness to accompany that reflects concern. It is his or her effectiveness in living that enables "touching" the helpee at the deepest level and to make a difference.

The Helper's Crisis

The crisis for the helpee, as can be seen, becomes the crisis for the helper. Whether or not the helper acknowledges it and attends to it does not make it the less so. If the helper can handle these crises, both he and the helpee can arrive at new levels of understanding and action. In the following excerpt, a 20-year-old male helpee, functioning at low levels, confronts the helper with the product of his fantasies. During the previous contact, in a moment of panic for the helpee, the helper had reached out both of his hands to hold the shaking helpee. The helpee, now distant from the earlier experience, denounces the helper:

Helpee: You . . . you're a dirty . . . seducer.

Helper: It's worse than that, isn't it?

Helpee: Yes! A homo! You're a dirty homosexual. (Silence) Well, I don't know. Maybe I want to seduce you.

Helper: You want to make a connection in some way.

Helpee: (Weeping) I never could love anyone. They wouldn't let my love in and now I have no outlet for my feelings.

Helper: Except now—with me.

Helpee: Maybe you're strong enough to accept it.

Helper: You're hopeful because you want my strength—my potency. You want so much to be able to live, to act, to love. You want to choose life.

Because the helper is unafraid to enter forbidden areas about forbidden impulses, the helpee is able to express himself fully. Together, they are able to arrive at the meaning behind the impulses, meaning that can be translated into constructive action.

Although the crisis that initiates the helping process is the helpee's, many of the crises along the way will be shared by both the helper and helpee. Depending on the wholeness of the helpee, the helper may carry the major part of the burden in many instances. Consider the moment when both the helper and helpee are richly laden with emotional insights but have not yet discovered the essential, final direction of helping. The question for both is "What are you going to do with the insights?" or "What are we going to do with our insights?" It is the neurotic hope that insight is sufficient and that action is unnecessary. It is the neurotic desire to rely upon constructs rather than construction. It's the helper's crisis as well as the helpee's.

Similarly, the termination of helping is sometimes more of a crisis for the helper than it is for the helpee. Or, put another way, it is as much of a crisis for the helper as it is for the helpee. The end of effective helping should involve handling no different from the handling of any other crisis. The helpee must go out into the real world, and the helper must let him go. Most often, this is difficult for the helper who has not given fully of himself—who has to discharge all of his responsibilities to the helpee. It is very difficult for the helper who does not trust himself or herself and does not trust what he or she has done in helping. It is even more difficult for the helper who is not himself living effectively, for he cannot trust the helpee to live effectively upon leaving helping. He fears for the helpee as he fears for himself, for he, the helper, cannot choose. Often, whereas the first crisis is the helpee's, the last crisis is the helper's.

In transition, here is what we know about helpees in **"The Relating Crisis"**:

The Relating Crisis

- Helpees will be impacted by crises introduced by unempathic helpers (e.g., crises in the helpers' lives will influence the helpees')
- High-level functioning helpees will be less traumatically impacted by helper-introduced process crises.
- Low-level functioning helpees will be traumatically impacted by helper-introduced process crises.

3

The Facilitators

When we write about crises, we are not simply concerned with the crises in the past or the present of the helpee. We are writing about crises that occur for the helper as well as the helpee, and between helpee and helper, both in and out of helping.

A typical crisis might be introduced by the helpee. In a series of experimental studies, unknown to the helper involved, a female helpee was given training and a **"mental set"** to explore herself deeply during the first third of an interview, to talk only about irrelevant and impersonal details during the middle third, and to explore herself deeply again during the final third of the interview. Thus, the helpee experimentally introduced a "crisis" for the helper. After the helpee was exploring herself deeply and meaningfully, she suddenly "runs away" from therapy and the helper loses contact with her. Whatever he does, he should not be able to bring her back to high levels of helping process movement. The communication process, for which he is largely responsible, has broken down.

The results are thought provoking. In a way similar to the pattern of the high-level-functioning helpees, during the experimental period of the helpee-introduced crisis the helper functioning at high levels functions independently of the helpee during the middle period. There is a tendency for those functioning at the highest levels to increase the level of conditions that they offer when the helpee lowers her self-exploration. On the other hand, those helpers functioning at low levels dropped their conditions precipitously when the helpee experimentally lowered her depth of self-exploration. However, unlike the pattern of the low-level helpees in the experimental manipulation of helper-offered conditions, during the final period when the helpee again explored herself deeply, **the helpers never again offered conditions even close to the level of those they had offered initially.**

Perhaps many of the significant results of the study may be best portrayed by the helpee's illustration of her experience and her character sketches of the helpers involved:

> Recently I took part in a fascinating research project involving the manipulation of several helpers by a helpee. I was the helpee who attempted the manipulation by presenting a problem and exploring as deeply as possible for the first 20 minutes of the hour, then suddenly switching off to irrelevancies such as the weather, the décor of the office, and again after 20 minutes of chit chat, suddenly, going back into deep exploration of my problem. The object was to test the ability of the helpers to bring the helpee back in the middle section into contact with the emotional implications of the problem.
>
> To give a clearer understanding of the project, I am a middle-aged woman who recently had enrolled at a large university as a graduate student. During the first semester I had had a brief chance to counsel an undergraduate student, with the sessions taped so that they might be a learning experience for me. My reaction upon hearing the tapes was not the expected one of hearing missed cues, but rather one of surprise and dismay at the personality I heard when I listened to myself. This, then, was the problem that I presented to each of the eight helpers whom I subsequently saw. Since none of the helpers had ever seen me before, I was, for them, apparently just another helpee coming for help. Each session was taped, and this was accomplished in a routine way. Thus, a real problem was presented by a legitimate helpee, and it was a genuine test of what happens to the helper when the helpee attempts to control the hour.

The following excerpts typify the functioning of the high-level helper during the three periods of the research:

Period 1

Helpee: As you may know, I heard my first tape and it threw me for a real loop as to whether I should go into counseling because I came across as a different person from what I ever thought of myself as being. I came out a weak, defensive, whiny old lady, and what worries me is, am I this person to begin with or is this just something superficial in my way of projecting myself? Or, you know, am I fit to counsel, because I wouldn't go to anybody who sounded like that myself?

Helper: You are saying, "My God, is that the real me?"

Helpee: Yeah, that was exactly what I said.

Helper: Sounds like it was something that, bang, hit you, and almost knocked you down.

Helpee: For about two weeks it really threw me, but then I got to thinking, well, maybe it was a habit, some way of speaking that I'd learned and that it was interfering and was not the real me. And I don't know whether that's rationalizing, you know, or whether—I'm in a quandary now whether I continue counseling—it has a lot to do with it—you know, if something's there I can unlearn and project in a different way, okay, but if I'm weak I have no business counseling others. And besides, I don't want to think of myself as this kind of a person because it's the kind of person I don't like.

Helper: I get two messages from you. One is that this thing was a helluva shock to you, to hear your own voice, to hear what you thought you were in this interview, and I get another message from you, which, at another level, you're protesting that you're not really a weak, whiny old lady.

Even during the second period, the high-level-functioning helper was able to relate seemingly irrelevant material to personally meaningful experiences of the helpee. After all, her choice of irrelevant and impersonal material was in some way personal, and the helper stretched to tune in on its meaning. It was very difficult indeed for the helpee to maintain her mental set.

Period 2

Helpee: That reminds me, there's something about this town. It's an awfully cold town. Northerners are so blasted—uh—indifferent. Or I don't know, they're certainly not very warm or easy to know. I've been here since last summer, and I swear I don't know anybody at all.

Helper: It's hard to know where you stand, at some deep level you feel very much lost and alone or cut off.

Helpee: Well, I think these professors particularly have their own little circles and nobody, you know . . .

Helper: You're so disappointed because there's no room . . .

Helpee: And nobody entertains much apparently, except within the department or something of that sort, and they have their own interests, the townspeople have their own interests, and the kids are busy studying and they have their little group, and I'm a grandma to them. And still there's not much you can do about this, but it is different from Washington. I was in this house here for two weeks before anyone even said, "Hello, you know, I'm a neighbor. How are you?" And finally one neighbor stopped in to borrow a stick of butter and then I didn't see anyone else for another two weeks.

Helper: You're really asking, "Does anyone around here really care?"

Finally, during the third part of the session, the helpee returned again to explore herself at relatively high levels.

Period 3

Helpee: I did that for years and years, trying to be what someone else wanted me to be, but I thought I was over that . . .

Helper: You keep telling me "I'm not what my voice is. I'm a volcano."

Helpee: But I never associated my voice as being anything but . . .

Helper: You keep telling me you're not what you appear to be. You know what you've told me this hour—you've told me, "I look like I'm meek, but I'm not."

Helpee: I'm a lion, not a mouse.

Helper: Your voice changed a little bit when you said that. It was looser.

Helpee: Uh hum . . .

Helper: You could get pretty angry at that. "I'm not a mouse." What did you feel when you said that?

Helpee: I felt like roaring.

Helper: You're damn right you did. Wish you did— "Don't you call me a mouse."

(continued)

Period 3 *(concluded)*

Helpee: Oh, yeah, many a time.

Helper: I'm a mouse and a mouse can't help anybody. Lions can. Oh, I don't know— constructive lions can, lions who can make discriminations about when it is appropriate to raise your voice.

Helpee: Hmm, I hadn't thought of that.

Helper: To be human I have to be able to communicate my anger and my joy *and* everything in between. And inside I know these things. I know these experiences inside. Huh? I've got to make discriminations about when it's appropriate to show these feelings, and by God, counseling is an appropriate place.

We may view the helper's levels of relating to the helpee's expressions in Figure 3-1.

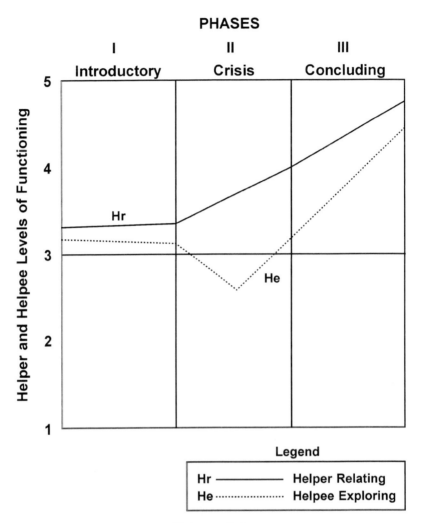

PHASES

Figure 3-1.
High Levels of Relating to Helpee Crisis

As may be noted, the helper began with high levels of empathic responsiveness and never abandoned this responsiveness during the experimental "crisis" period. Indeed, he actually elevated his levels of responsiveness during the crisis, and he introduced still higher levels of responsive initiative during the latter part of the session. He was a true Facilitator.

Helpees in Crisis

The obvious example of helping in crisis involves some critical moment in the life of the helpee where what he does or does not do will lead him toward more full emergence or deterioration. Thus, in the following excerpt, the male helpee, who is an executive in his 40s functioning at low levels, presents the very real and immediate crisis of his life. In particular, note how the helper responds consistently to the feeling and meaning of the helpee's experience:

Helpee: I just can't go on anymore. Oh, no! I just can't go in each day.

Helper: You're down because you don't see any way up or out.

Helpee: I've had it. I think it's going to end each day. I live in fear of not making it through each day. It's unbearable.

Helper: It's so hopeless you're not sure you want to face another day.

Helpee: It's too much, I don't think I can take any more. I'm out of it already.

Helper: You're scared because you don't think you've got what it takes to make it through.

Helpee: I know I don't. I'm more than scared, I'm all the way down.

Helper: You're beat because life is just too much for you and you can't handle it all.

Helpee: I can't handle anything: my wife, family, job. Can't even talk to people—and they don't understand.

Helper: You feel alone because you can't reach those who mean the most to you.

Helpee: I used to—I want to, but I just hurt them and then feel guilty and ugly.

Helper: You're frightened because you can't maintain contact with those you love and you want to tell them how much they mean to you.

In this case, when the helper realizes that his helpee is "at the end of his rope," the helper responds empathically to that experience first. Then the helper initiates to identify what the helpee experiences as missing and moves the helpee toward filling the gap with a skill. Crises are crises because the individual has no response to deal with a situation. The larger the repertoire of responses available, the fewer the crises the individual experiences.

What constitutes a crisis for some may not be for others. The external crises for the helpee may range from something as apparently innocuous as concern for an impending class-room presentation to the moment of contemplating suicide. For some, the most innocuous may merge with the most serious. Thus, for example, the severe stutterer who has had a traumatic experience in a previous presentation and who, in some way, sees his or her future resting upon his or her next performance, may consider the very serious consequences of a disastrous classroom experience. We can see most clearly the essential character of the crisis: whether physical or psychological, it is of life-and-death urgency.

In addition, there may be crises that occur during the helping process itself. During the initial phase of helping, the helpee's growing feeling that the helper cannot under-stand him or her may constitute a crisis of minor or major proportions, depending on the desperateness of the helpee's situation and the ability of the helper to handle the crisis. For the deteriorated schizophrenic who is the product of a series of severely retarding relationships, the helping encounter may offer the last promise of hope. He or she may make a feeble attempt to reach out for help. Whether or not the helper can understand him is indeed of life-and-death urgency.

An example of a potentially critical moment during helping might involve the helper's inability to enable the helpee to find direction: that is, having explored intensely and extensively as far as he can go, the helpee is not able, in his relationship with the helper, to establish a meaningful direction for his life's activities. Again, depending on both the helpee's and the helper's levels of development, the consequences may be constructive or deteriorative.

Also neglected are the crises that occur both in and out of therapy for the helper, both alone and in his interaction with the helpee. Thus, occurrences in the helper's own life situation and experiences in his relationships may constitute crises for the helper.

For example, marital difficulties or a lack of sexual fulfillment might have a critical effect on the helper interacting with a sexually attractive helpee and could create a crisis in therapy. Within the helping process itself, the moment when the helper has "lost" the helpee, when he or she is no longer in communication with the helpee—perhaps at a difficult moment for the latter—constitutes a severe crisis point for the helper.

The only real helping takes place at the crisis point. Most often, helpers focus initially on external crises for the helpee but eventually on crises involving both the helpee and the helper, both in and out of helping. At the crisis point, both helpee and helper are stripped of all facades, which is indicated by what they do or do not do. This communication is the most intimate person-to-person communication there can be. Although there are no fixed "rules" for responding to the crisis, the helper's goals are the same as when he or she is learning: explore in order to understand a goal, and then develop an action program to achieve the goal. Often developing a personalized goal with and for the helpee is enough to gain the time needed to increase the quality and quantity of the helpee's repertoire of physical, emotional, and intellectual responses. The helper's response reflects her recognition of the life-and-death urgency of the situation. *She responds the way she lives her life, and she chooses life in her response.* In his or her "being" and acting, he or she discloses the meaning and efficacy of his or her approach to life.

The first stage in crisis helping is an acknowledgment of the crisis by the helper. He cannot turn away from the crisis. Yet many helpers do turn away from the crisis point. Those helpers functioning at low levels cannot clearly see the life-and-death urgency through the helpee's eyes. They cannot experience his or her desperation. They cannot allow themselves to do so. Perhaps most importantly, they are not aware that anyone at a crisis point can choose life. In their deterministic view of man, they do not, in effect, believe in the possibility of change. These people do not understand the privilege of helping another because they no longer believe in the possibility of change or growth. They deny change and growth because they are so caught up in their own needs that they can no longer act but can only react.

The helper functioning at low levels does not approach being whole himself. *He is not and cannot be aware.* He emphasizes in helping, as he does in real life, the irrelevant details, the "in-between" stuff. The implications are profound. *If* helping begins at the crisis point and *if* the helper functioning at low levels can neither acknowledge nor cope with the crisis, then **with the helpee functioning at low levels, there is no real helping.** While there may be helpee movement from the absence of effective communication to distorted communication from a distorted perceptual base, there is no real self-sustaining and effective communication.

If there is time at the crisis point—and often there is not—the helper may choose to proceed cautiously, and rightfully and meaningfully so. If there is little time, as is most often the case, the helper must move in quickly to clear away the "crud," the irrelevancies that cloud the critical issues for the helpee. In any event, whether there is time or not, the helper must ultimately **"touch"** the helpee, letting him know that he is with the helpee in the helpee's deepest, most desperate moments.

"Touching" is, in effect, accurate responding to the feeling and the meaning of what the helpee communicates. Touching is relieving the confusion by providing a personally relevant goal for the helpee.

If the helpee cannot communicate his desperate circumstances or if he cannot allow his full experience of the crisis to emerge within him, the **"whole helper"** may precipitate the crisis by confrontation or other means. **The whole helper can experience the helpee more than the helpee can experience himself.** The whole helper can enable the helpee to face squarely the life-and-death issues before her and thus enable the helpee to take her first steps toward or back to life. *If both helper and helpee allow it to happen, helping represents an hourly intensification of life in all of its crises and all of its fulfillment.*

In transition, here is what we know about the Facilitator.

The Facilitator

- Whatever else he does, the helper will always attempt to be accurately empathic in order to facilitate your exploration of your experience.

- Whatever else he does, the helper will always attempt to personalize your "ownership" of your experience in order to facilitate your understanding of new goals in your life.

- Whatever else he does, the helper will initiate with you to develop individualized action programs to achieve the goals in your life.

The results of the encounter with the Facilitator may best be summarized in the helpee's own words:

> The helper walked in and I saw a man who looked shorter than he is with a brush of black hair tinged with gray, big wide eyes under bushy brows, the eyes the main feature. Something in those eyes makes you feel safe, and yet you know he can really think. But you know the guy has feelings by those eyes—none of those cold empty eyes. He talks in a voice so big it almost scares you, but not rough and not smooth, but gentle, though big. He could blast you right out of your chair, but he probably wouldn't. Somehow I know I could trust him. And so I started telling him how it is with me, and he seems to be right with me all the time. I don't know, but it's as if he didn't even need my words and I didn't feel as if he was faking. Oh, some of the time I felt he was bored waiting for me to spell it out because he was ahead of me, not because he thought I wasn't worth his time. He had a way of putting my words into such specific and marvelous analogies that made me feel more deeply what it was I only vaguely was aware of before. He gave off vitality and allowed me to share it—not that I left him with less but that he had so much and he was allowing me to take what I needed. He made me feel as if I was OK and would be able to use it usefully and come out of it. He gave me hope, optimism, and a more clearly defined problem than when I went in.

4

The Retarders

Facilitators are rare. Without facilitative human development—including, in particular, modeling parents and parental surrogates—facilitators are absent altogether. Without systematic training in relating skills, would-be helpers cannot offer empathic relating skills. Human crises simply drive them to dissemble in many different ways.

Witness, for example, in the study of helpee-introduced crises, the results were quite varied. Again, during the initial period, the helpee presented essentially the same difficulty.

Period 1

Helpee: I have a problem. My problem began some time ago.

Helper: Say, I don't believe I got your name.

Helpee: Oh, Janie, Janie Clark.

Helper: Janie Clark. Thank you. You know who I am?

Helpee: Yeah, Dr. Jones.

Helper: Yeah, Dr. Jones, yeah.

Helpee: Anyway, I had my first counseling session and it was taped, and when I turned on the tape to hear the cues I'd missed and things, and I didn't hear anything except my voice and the way I came across as a person. And at the time, it really threw me for a loop because I'd never thought of myself as the kind of person that I came across as on the tape. It wasn't just, you know, the different

---

(continued)

Period 1 *(continued)*

Helper: sound of the voice, or anything like that. It was a whole new me, you know, a different me, and I didn't know whether it was just that I'd picked up ways of expressing myself, which I told myself at first, but I didn't like what I saw, obviously. I came out a very weak, whiny, pathetic little old lady, and I'd never thought of myself that way. And there it was just clearly, that was all that was coming across.

Helper: This is your interpretation of the—uh—your listening to yourself on the tape. You thought you were not as strong a character perhaps.

Helpee: Nothing!

Helper: In other words, a difference in yourself.

Helpee: A blobby sort of a—no personality, no umpf, no nothing that you could relate to.

Helper: And you, you think this is—and what do you think, perhaps, the tape is a true indication of the—of your interpretation . . .

Helpee: Yeah, my first reaction was that maybe I'd learned to express myself poorly but then finally I realized that no, this was a part of me that I just never had recognized that was coming out and, this is a very recent thing for me to be willing to admit that, you know, that this is me.

(Silence)

(continued)

Period 1 *(concluded)*

Helper: I have talked about it with a number of people and that undoubtedly has helped me to recognize that—I'm still pretty hung up on some of it, though, I'm so used to thinking of myself in certain ways—partly I can be totally unconscious of this and then afterwards I think, oh, there was that dear little old lady again, and, apparently, there are some aspects of the dear little old lady that I still think I like.

Helper: Uh, huh.

Helpee: But I don't like the total picture at all, not at all.

Helper: So, you know it gives you a sort of a negative picture of yourself.

During the second period, the helpee was able to manipulate the helper successfully. The discussion was on her terms, and indeed, in many ways the helper appeared to feel more comfortable.

Period 2

Helpee: And I like the Northeast, and so they said, "Well, try this state," and so that's all I knew. And so then I came up here.

Helper: Now you're enrolled in the Master's program?

Helpee: Yes.

Helper: Are you teaching, too?

(continued)

Period 2 *(continued)*

Helpee: No.

Helper: You have a teaching certificate?

Helpee: No.

Helper: What did you major in at college?

Helpee: Political science. Big help.

Helper: A general college education.

Helpee: Yeah. Oh, I love the weather up here now. I'm dreading the summer because someone told me it's hot. Part of the reason I came up here was because Washington summers are unbearable. But they tell me it gets real hot here. You probably would love some good hot weather, coming from the North, as you said.

Helper: No, I like cool weather.

Helpee: Yeah, I hate the thought of thinking of myself as the kind of person who anybody can say "boo" to and I'll turn around and run.

Helper: Yeah.

Helpee: I never understood how you guys got up here in this hall.

Helper: More room.

Helpee: Well, I thought it was because you guys must be in bad repute, and so they sent you to this old building.

(continued)

Period 2 *(concluded)*

Helper: I don't know about that part of it, but the ostensible reason is more room.

Helpee: It's pretty dilapidated, but it is kind of off to itself. The other building is so busy.

Helper: Yeah, it's crowded.

Finally, the helpee again returns to relatively high levels of self-exploration, but the helper does not quite return to the level at which he was functioning during the first period of the study.

Period 3

Helpee: To me fighting is a dirty word—somehow it means hurting people, getting hurt, you know, there's nothing healthy or good about it—seems awful to have to fight.

Helper: When people fight you, you get hurt, so you don't want to.

Helpee: Well . . .

Helper: You don't want to fight other people so you won't hurt them.

Helpee: I don't want to hurt or get hurt. It's a combination of all these things, and I don't want any part of it—but I don't like the other alternative which is to . . .

(continued)

Period 3 *(continued)*

Helper: The reality I guess, in the best sense, you'd like to avoid a fight, that is, if it's your way— but in real life, people have differences of opinion, so this is where you're hung up, so you'll either have to fight for your say or else you don't get it.

Helpee: You know I might just as well not have had the fight. I would feel very defeated if I went in and fought and lost.

Helper: You mean you might feel more defeated than you feel now.

Helpee: Yeah, that's right.

Helper: You wouldn't feel that if you fought and lost.

Helpee: I identify fighting with losing.

Helper: I see. So you think you win a fight?

Helpee: When you get in a fight, you either win or lose, and I'm the loser.

Helper: Huh.

Helpee: I always have been, and I just always expect to be.

Helper: Which to me it seems sort of that in a sense you're defeated before you start. You're certainly not going to win the battle if you don't fight, uh, unless you're lucky, maybe, and it just sort of falls that way.

(continued)

> **Period 3** *(concluded)*
>
> **Helpee:** But somehow it doesn't seem as much of a defeat if you, you know, I chose to walk off, and I haven't lost face, or something. I don't know, but if I fight, then my self-esteem goes down.

Note that the helper never made an accurate response to the feeling or meaning of the helpee's expressions. This was particularly true when the helpee withdrew from meaningful exploration during Period 2 and the helper drifted away to oblivion.

The declining pattern is one that most low-level-functioning helpers present over a number of sessions of helping. That is, it would appear that following the exercising of the initial repertoire of responses during the early sessions, with the helpee's continuing presentation of crises, whether acknowledged by the helper or not, the low-level-functioning helpers deteriorate in functioning over helping.

In the study, the would-be helpers' efforts followed the modal pattern of experimentally manipulated helpee exploration (see Figure 4-1). As may be viewed, in the initial phase, the modal pattern began with their optimal performances; all declined in performance during the middle crisis phase. While some recovered slightly in the third phase of helping, none recovered to the level at which they began.

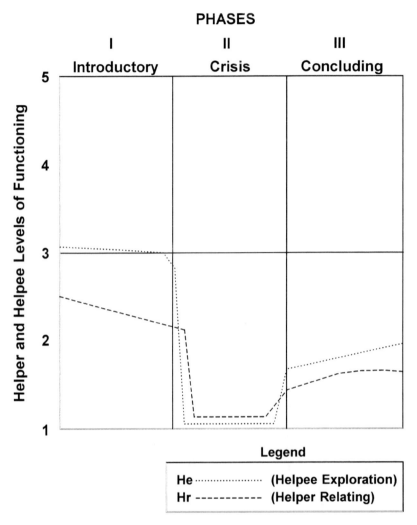

Figure 4-1.
Modal Levels of Relating to Helpee Crises

At a minimum, this means that all would-be helpers were manipulated by the helpee crisis: in effect, they were exposed as incompetents, lacking the skill necessary to manage the crisis. At a maximum, this means that the would-be helpers were **"caught up"** in their own crises, never again to even pretend to be **"apparently helpful."** In effect, the would-be helpers are exposed to themselves as legitimate **"helpees,"** internalizing ownership for their own inabilities to manage the crises.

Those would-be helpers who continue to pretend to be helpful are now psychopathically committed to subtracting from all expressions of the helpee's experience. A sustained interaction with such a retarder will lead to the deterioration of helpee functioning—physically, emotionally, intellectually. We label this experience **"The Sucabus":** it is as if the Retarder takes a gram of food away with each encounter until the helpee starves to death.

The helpee's impressions of her experience are related as follows:

I must mention that as an inexperienced layman, I had anticipated that I would learn a bit more about myself, particularly in
regard to the techniques, from these experienced helpers. I had
absolutely no forewarning that I would be so appalled at the
destructiveness of some of the helpers nor that I would be so
excited by the facilitative one. I had not really envisioned that
there would be a difference that I could so easily detect. After
all, these were highly trained, experienced helpers, each of
whom counseled several helpees daily. My first impressions
were, in all but one case, validated by the replaying of the taped
sessions. In this particular case, I think I was misled by the fact
that this was a woman helper, and being a woman, I probably
unconsciously hoped to see a good helper and therefore must
have given her the benefit of the doubt. She also was bright and
intelligent, and it was only after playing back the tape that I could
see that her intelligence was misused and could not be trusted.
But in all other cases, I sensed immediately whether the helper
was showing respect and genuine interest in me as a human
being or merely reciting a litany, so to speak. With the facilitative
one, I came away feeling that I had had a glimpse of a real
human being in a genuine encounter, and that this person had
some understanding and appreciation of me as a human being.
I felt that I had learned and could learn more about myself and
life from this individual and was, therefore, hopeful of finding a
better way of living. With the others, I came away feeling that the
helper had been totally indifferent to me and to my needs, either
because of his own needs, or because he was incapable of
feeling for me, that I had not only learned nothing from the
encounter, but also that I left feeling very depressed and hopeless. This occurred with several helpers in a greater or lesser
degree. With some of them, I felt sympathy—with others, I felt
disgust and anger that they should be allowed to be in a so-called
"helping" profession. I could only think of a really sick person
who had finally worked up the courage to make perhaps one
last attempt to find a human being with enough love and
understanding to help him find his way out of his misery. I was
appalled to think of his winding up with some of these inadequate
counselors who would surely destroy his last hope. It seemed to
me criminal negligence on the part of society to allow this kind of
helper to operate.

In addition to the facilitative helper, the helpee provided the following character sketches of each of the other helpers:

Helper 2

Helper 2 was a slight, blondish, watery-eyed person whom you wouldn't ordinarily ever remember seeing. He had absolutely no presence, but he had a Ph.D. With this helper, within a few sentences, I could hardly wait to get to the part where I could talk about nothing at all. He absolutely floored me when he asked a lot of irrelevant questions about my husband's salary, my status, and so on. I wanted to tell him what those questions did to me—I wound up just despising him, and unconsciously this came out. When I listened to the tape, I heard myself give a very destructive laugh. I had definitely written him off within the first two minutes, and the only reason I stayed was to do the research, but I would never have returned to this man if I had needed help of any kind.

Helper 3

Helper 3 was a big, blondish, sunny type of southern fellow. He was a genuinely warm guy and a very likeable one. He exuded friendliness and his eyes sparkled. You got a feeling he could really enjoy a good laugh. I did not feel that he pressed hard enough on my problems. I thought I liked him. He seemed too slow-paced and I didn't think his intellect was as sharp as some. But I felt that I didn't really know him in any sense and that he was holding back because he didn't know me yet.

Helper 4

I felt as if Helper 4 was trying and wanted to be helpful, but I found it difficult to react to his personality. He was an older but sort of nondescript-looking man, smoked a pipe, and looked possibly scholarly. He immediately indicated he was not feeling up to par, and I felt I wanted to be nice to him because I felt sorry for him, but did not want to for my own sake. However, I felt he was reaching out to me, but sort of for my help. It was easy to talk about him as against myself but that seems a part of getting to know him. I did not feel interested in going back to him, though.

(continued)

Helper 5

Helper 5 seemed pretty stiff and intellectual and gave the impression of really knowing her stuff and of having had to battle hard to wrench any of what she knew out of men—almost a caricature of a career girl. But she had a soft voice and smiled brightly and made me feel as if she was on my side against the men in this world. She didn't actually say anything about men, so far as I can remember, but somehow I picked up the feeling that she was strange and different. It was easy to get her to talk about her pictures and books, which surprised me as I had expected her by her appearance to be tougher. I came away thinking she was really bright and knew about helping. After listening to the tapes, she came out the most boring, the least interested, and not very bright. I am still puzzled as to what made me think she was bright, as I am not usually fooled that easily. My only thought is that I projected my need to see a woman helper as good.

Helper 6

Helper 6 was a big, burly, black-haired, beetle-browed, soft-fat ethnic-looking man who might do manual labor rather than have a Ph.D. in psychology. He was a typical client-centered helper—fed me back my words until I wanted to say: "Haven't you any ideas of your own?" and "That's what I said, what are you saying them for?" It annoyed me very much, and I could hardly refrain from mentioning it. I felt he wasn't really very interested in my problem, but it was his job to sit there and be polite. My general feeling was one of annoyance with him. I would not go back if I had any problem. I came away from this interview feeling frustrated.

(continued)

Helper 7

This poor woman surprised me in being better than I had anticipated. Helper 7 looked like a tousled, slipshod sort of matron with no organization to her character or mind. She actually was a better helper than the neat, efficient woman I had seen before. She was touched by my problem because it coincided in some respects with hers, and soon I felt that I should be helping her. It was, in fact, very difficult for me to remember that I was there for research purposes and that I shouldn't, therefore, exchange roles with her during this hour. She made me feel very sad and depressed, and yet I liked her and wished I could cheer her up. She would not be able to help you grow, but could give directions for specific problems, and they would probably be oriented toward her own philosophy and her own problems. But she was herself more than some of the others.

Helper 8

Helper 8 was a long, lanky, dark-haired, really blue-eyed, tall, stringbean of a man: young. I felt immediately a sense of intellect that was a relief after some of the others. I wasn't sure if he could be warm. As he talked, he seemed warm, but I had a tiny part of me saying, "I'm not sure I'd like to get in a fight with him." I felt he might not be on my side if I didn't show up well. He was very sharp, and it was extremely difficult to pull him away from my problem. I was very depressed when I went in to see him, and he seemed to want to help me get over this depression and I felt that he probably could. During this hour, though, I was unable to shake off the depressions, which I felt was because I was unwilling rather than because he could not help me. I felt that if I went back to him and really put myself on the line, he could unravel a hell of a lot of my problems for me, but I'm not sure I'd go back unless I felt especially courageous at the time. He might not go all the way with me if I showed something he didn't like or couldn't feel. It was just a matter of not feeling 100 percent safe. I felt him to be strong enough, but perhaps not tender enough.

These excerpts are classic in their depiction of many important aspects of relating or absence thereof. First, the dependence of the low-level-functioning conditioned reactor helper is in contrast to the independence of the thinking helper. Second, the helpee-manipulated excerpts and her descriptions place in sharp relief the difference between those who choose to die and ask others to die with them and those who choose life and ask others to choose life with them. Those who choose death at the crisis point do everything they can to make others choose to die. Those who choose life do everything they can to make others choose to live. Those who choose to die do so because they have closed themselves to new experiences. They live the same experience day in and day out because they cannot respond to anything or anyone. Those who choose life do so because they are open to new experiences. They have different experiences day after day because they can respond to anything or anyone when it is appropriate and they learn. Because they learn, they have fewer and fewer crises.

The helpee's descriptions of the helpers involved remains for us congruent with our experience and research as well as reflecting the helpee's experience. Those who can deliver results tell us early and sustain their efforts with energy, direction, and discipline—those who can help use time well and those who cannot help waste time. At the crisis, the low-level helpers lose all semblance of direction and never return to their previous levels of functioning, however brief and poor to begin with. The high-level-functioning helper actually increased his levels of functioning at the point of crisis.

In transition, if it is to occur at all, relating must be done by high-level-functioning people. What others do is some sort of twisted game without even the appearance of decency. It is sick and cruel. The low-functioning helpers are as much failures in their lives as they are in helping. It can be no other way. They emphasize the irrelevant, personally and profes- sionally, while they ignore the fabric of life woven from the learnings that emerge from the work and the skill it takes to meet and resolve crises.

In summary, we have learned a great deal about what it means to not be facilitative in helping.

The Retarder

• Whatever else he does, the would-be helper will never observe enough to "see" and listen enough to "hear" in order to be responsive in facilitating your exploration of your experience.

• Whatever else he does, the would-be helper will never help you personalize your experience in order to facilitate your understanding of new goals in your life.

• Whatever else he does, the would-be helper will help you initiate to develop individualized action programs to achieve the goals in your life.

In transition, helping provides the helpee with the empathic relating conditions necessary for the acquisition of responses and skills the helpee did not have. Again, the effective helper provides the conditions necessary for learning. These conditions involve the appropriate use of responsive and initiative skills that, in turn, facilitate helpee exploration, understanding, and action. A crisis may or may not be a structure within which the helpee and helper can learn, grow, and initiate constructively. Whether it is or not depends on the repertoire of skills the helper commands.

The helper handles the crisis or not as he or she is a whole person or not. There are rules for functioning in unknown areas, and they involve energy, organization, direction, and systematic action as well as full vigilance from the helper so that he or she may explore, understand, and act.

The truly tragic outcome is this: confronted with a crisis, not of their own making, **most would-be helpers demonstrate profiles similar to those of their helpees.** Not only do they have nothing to offer their helpees, they are sentenced to the same aimless existence of their helpees; as long as they continue the helper-façade, they will accelerate their own decline.

Those who choose to die, helpers as well as helpees, have an incredible number of strategies designed to help them die, and they all involve reacting. Those who choose to live have only one strategy to live, and it emphasizes empathy.

5

Facilitators and Retarders

We can also direct our empathic relating skills to social issues. The great issues of our times are fraught with complexity and often danger. So are the little issues! Indeed, the little issues are part of the cumulative effects that yield the great issues. Unattended, unresponded to, the cumulative effects of the little issues may be monstrous. Big bombs from many little bombs are made!

For example, since 9/11, the great issues of the twenty-first century have centered on **"World War III—The War Against Terror."** To be sure, the greatest of all issues is the fear of **"Home-Grown Terrorists."** Yet we have been implementing a systematic **"Design for Failure"** in our own inner cities.

Instead of responding empathically to relate to our inner-city youth, we have been ignoring them. Instead of initiating to empower them, we have been passive. Instead of freeing them, we have been attempting to control them.

- No one responds to the experience of inner-city youth:

  "You feel furious because you have been cheated of your rights to the full American experience."

- No one personalizes the experience of their hopelessness:

  "You feel hopeless because you cannot manage to set things right for yourself."

- No one initiates to objectify goals for their future:

  "You feel hopeful to find your own objectives, and you're eager to get started."

Because no one relates to the youth, here is how this **"Design for Failure"** works (see Figure 5-1).

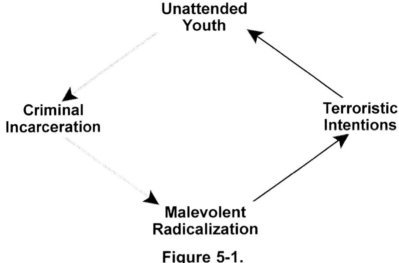

Figure 5-1.
The Design for Failure

This **"Design for Failure"** unfolds very simply:

- Because no one in the community responds empathically to unattended youth, they drift toward delinquent behavior.

- Because no one in the community initiates sensitively on behalf of the youth, many are incarcerated for criminal violations.

- Because no one in the prisons responds and initiates to protect the vulnerable youth, they are converted to radicalism by malevolent forces.

- Because no one in the community responds and initiates to prepare the youth for the return to the community, they return with terroristic intentions.

This simple design guarantees the presence of **"Home-Grown Terrorist Cells."** These **"Home-Grown Terrorists"** are, themselves, the products of the community's criminal neglect and inaction: nonresponsiveness and noninitiative in the face of urgent human needs for nourishment.

The Relationship of Responding and Initiating

Responding

We may begin by outlining the most urgent of requirements for facilitating human relating—empathic responding. The responding scale ranges from inattentiveness to responding by individualizing human experience (see Table 5-1). At the lowest levels, then, we are inattentive (Level 1) or barely attentive (Level 2) to another's experience. At the highest levels, we respond by personalizing (Level 4) and individualizing (Level 5) the other person's experience. At the threshold of responding (Level 3), we respond interchangeably to the feeling and meaning of another person's expression of their experience. Responding interchangeably to another's image of his or her experience is the minimal standard necessary for facilitative human relating.

Table 5-1.
Levels of Empathic Responsiveness

Levels	Behaviors
5	Responding by Individualizing
4	Responding by Personalizing
3	Responding Interchangeably
2	Attending to Appearance and Behavior
1	Nonattending

Initiating

We may continue by outlining the culminating requirement for facilitating human relating—initiating. The initiating scale ranges from nonorienting to initiating by technologizing programs (see Table 5-2). At the lowest levels, then, we are nonorienting (Level 1) or barely oriented toward a direction (Level 2). At the highest levels, we initiate by operationally defining an objective (Level 4) and technologically developing a program to achieve the objective (Level 5). At the threshold of initiating (Level 3), we initiate by concretizing directions. Concretizing directions is the minimal standard necessary for facilitative human relating.

Table 5-2.
Levels of Initiative

Levels		Behaviors
5	—	Initiating by Technologizing Programs
4	—	Initiating by Operationalizing Objectives
3	—	Initiating by Concretizing Directions
2	—	Orienting Toward Directions
1	—	Nonorienting

Relating

The relationship between responding and initiative dimensions is an independent one. This independence means that we have just as much of a chance of being high on one dimension and low on the other as we do of being high on one and high on the other. The relationship of the responding and initiative dimensions may be viewed in Figure 5-2. As may be noted, the dimensions bisect each other at right angles (Level 3). Above Level 3 are Levels 4 and 5. The higher levels meet the minimal standards for facilitative human relating. The lower levels do not.

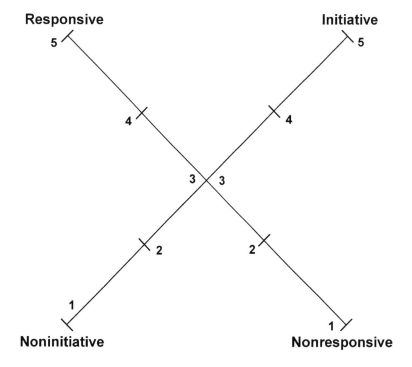

Figure 5-2.
The Relationship of
Responsive and Initiative Dimensions

The Light-Side and Dark-Side People

Armed with the independence of responding and initiative dimensions, we may now project images of the facilitators and the retarders (see Figure 5-3). By bisecting the responsive and initiative dimensions, we may define **"The Facilitators"** and **"The Retarders"**:

- **"The Facilitator"** is high on responsiveness and initiative.
- **"The Retarder"** is low on responsiveness and initiative.

This means that only **"The Facilitator"** adds to others by both understanding and acting. In turn, **"The Retarder"** subtracts from others by neither understanding nor acting.

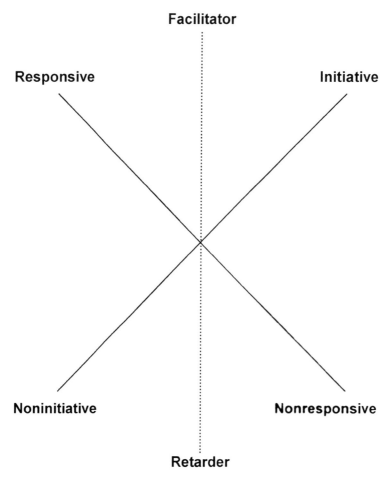

Figure 5-3.
Facilitators and Retarders

In turn, by bisecting the responsive and initiative dimensions, we may posit active and passive dimensions that further define **"Facilitators and Retarders"** (see Figure 5-4):

- **The Active Person** is nonresponsively initiative.
- **The Passive Person** is noninitiatively responsive.

These are incomplete people. The Active Person may harm by acting without understanding. The Passive Person may harm by not acting upon understanding.

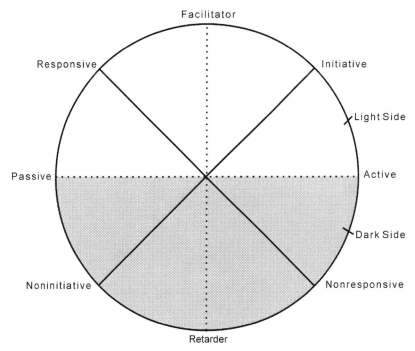

Figure 5-4.
Light-Side and Dark-Side People

By coloring in the lower half of the circle, we may give further meaning to the implications of **"The Facilitators and the Retarders"**:

- **Light-side people** are responsively initiative or initiatively responsive.

- **Dark-side people** are nonresponsive and noninitiative.

In short, at the highest levels, light-side people are **"The Facilitators."** In turn, at the lowest levels, dark-side people are **"The Retarders."**

What are the implications of these validated constructs— personal and social? The most powerful implication is that we can measure the dimensions of human relating and we are, therefore, accountable. Everything that we do in relation to others matters:

The Facilitators and the Retarders

- If we are high in responsive and initiative, we are **"Facilitators,"** and the people we serve will grow **"For Better."**
- If we are low in responsiveness and initiative, we are **"Retarders,"** and the people we serve will deteriorate **"For Worse."**

Relating to anyone as responsible helpers demands continuous responsiveness and initiative. Intervening in any cycle of failure requires accurate responsiveness culminating in programmatic initiatives.

Who are you? **Facilitator** or **Retarder? Light-side** or **Dark-side?**

6

Research and Development

The research on empathy and human relating began with the breakthrough insight of the **"interchangeability of responding"**:

> **Could one person (the helper) have communicated what the other person (the helpee) had communicated in terms of the feeling and meaning and the content of the expression?**

The interchangeable response enabled us to assess the effectiveness of all helping and human relationships.

What we discovered was astounding. Some helpers—parents, teachers, counselors, managers—never made an interchangeable response—**never, ever!** How, then, could they help others achieve their objectives? Other helpers—fewere than 5 of 100—would periodically check back with their helpees by making interchangeable responses all of the time.

The outcomes followed the processes. The helpees of helpers who made interchangeable responses improved on a whole variety of indices. The helpees of the **"pretend helpers"** who did not make interchangeable responses stayed the same or even declined on a variety of indices.

Again: **all learning begins with the learner's frame of reference.**

The ingredients of empathic relating evolved as we conducted further research in response to a number of challenges to the helping profession. In the process, we found that helping may be *"for better or for worse,"* that is, facilitative or retarding—a finding with significant implications for parents, teachers, counselors, therapists, managers, and the like. Moreover, we also discovered that we could account for the facilitative or retarding effects by the helpers' levels of functioning on certain scaled dimensions, such as empathic relating or responding.

It is worthwhile to view the models of relating that evolved through living, learning, and working applications associated with this research.

The Relating Models

The main effect of empathic relating on the part of the helper was to facilitate exploration of experience on the part of the helpee. With that, we had our first model for helping: *helper responding facilitates the helpee's experiential exploring of problems* (see Figure 6-1).

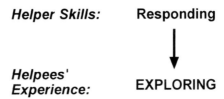

**Figure 6-1.
Early Model for Helping**

Eclectically drawing upon all theoretical orientations, we explored many scaled dimensions and then factor analyzed them. We discovered that these dimensions "loaded" upon two discrete interpersonal factors:

- Responding that emphasized empathy in relating to other people's frames of reference
- Initiating that emphasized helper genuineness in an empathic relationship.

With these results, we had a basic model for helping (see Figure 6-2):

- Responding facilitates exploring.
- Initiating stimulates acting.

The helpees could now act upon their explorations of experience.

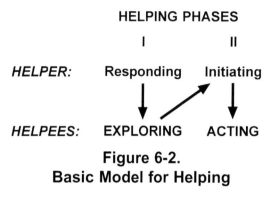

Figure 6-2.
Basic Model for Helping

Further requirements of the interpersonal dimensions yielded a transitional dimension between responding and initiating, based on the personalizing factor:

Personalizing that emphasized the immediacy of experiencing and internalizing, especially as it relates to responsibility for one's actions.

With that, the researchers had a transitional model for helping (see Figure 6-3):

> **Personalizing facilitates understanding.**

The helpees could now act based on their self-understanding.

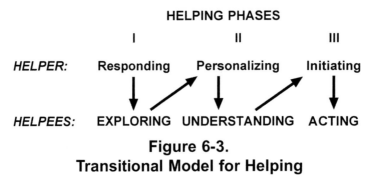

Figure 6-3.
Transitional Model for Helping

The comprehensive model was not completed until other factors were analyzed and incorporated. Foremost among these factors was attending:

Attending that emphasizes paying attention to others by attending physically, observing their appearance and behavior, and listening to their expressions of their experience

With that, the researchers had a comprehensive model for engaging or involving others in the helping process (see Figure 6-4):

- Attending facilitates involving.
- Responding facilitates exploring.
- Personalizing facilitates understanding.
- Initiating facilitates acting.

The helpers could now engage the helpees in a comprehensive helping process.

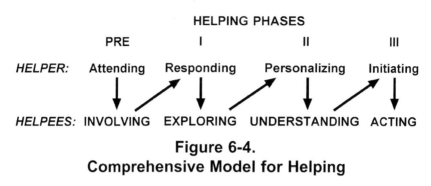

Figure 6-4.
Comprehensive Model for Helping

Finally, feedback is recycled for continuous and improved processing (see Figure 6-5):

- More intensive involving
- More extensive exploring
- More accurate understanding
- More effective acting

Both helpees and helpers now had a comprehensive model for continuous processing of increasingly productive responses.

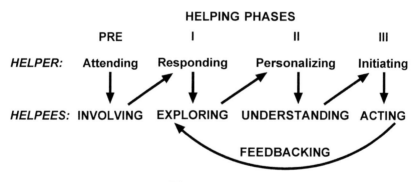

Figure 6-5.
Continuous Processing Model for Helping

Learning

With educational applications and analyses, the helping model was expanded to incorporate teaching skills (see Figure 6-6). As we may see:

- Content development plus attending facilitates involving.
- Diagnosing plus responding facilitates exploring.
- Learning objectives plus personalizing facilitates understanding.
- Individualizing learning programs plus initiating facilitates acting.

Again, feedback is recycled to facilitate a more productive teaching-learning process. Both teachers and learners could now implement a comprehensive model for learning.

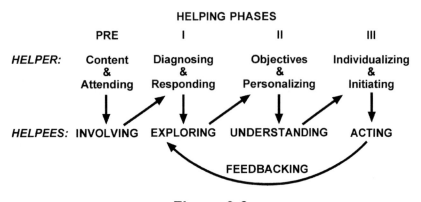

Figure 6-6.
Comprehensive Model for Teaching

Working

With working applications and analyses, the helping/teaching model was expanded to incorporate working and thinking skills (see Figure 6-7). As we may see:

> • Goaling plus content and attending facilitate involving.
>
> • Expanding plus diagnosing and responding facilitate exploring.
>
> • Narrowing plus objectives and personalizing facilitate understanding.
>
> • Programming plus individualizing and initiating facilitate acting.

Once again, feedback is recycled to facilitate the most productive working-thinking process. Managers and supervisors and workers now had a comprehensive model for working and thinking on the job.

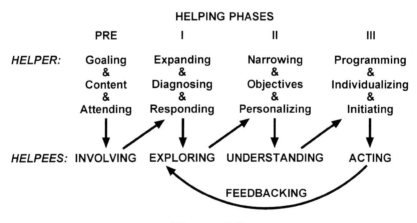

Figure 6-7.
Comprehensive Model for Working and Thinking

With our associates, we went on to make demonstrations of the effects of relating interventions in all areas of human experience: parenting, education, counseling, psychotherapy, and business/industry management and supervision.

Moreover, we made demonstrations of the effects of direct relating-skills training upon helpees in all areas of human experience: children, learners, counselees, patients, employees, and supervisees. In doing so, they introduced their principle of **"training as treatment"** or **"psychological education"** as a preferred model of treatment. Here is what the research yielded.

Process and Outcome

The effects of interpersonal-skills, or **IPS,** dimensions were summarized by the researchers in a review of 164 studies of more than 160,000 people. In this review, we find several sets of summary propositions drawn from these results as well as their processing-skills implications.

Summary Propositions

1. **The effects of helper interpersonal functioning upon recipient outcomes are positive and significant.**

   A summary of the effects of helpers upon helpee outcome indices suggests that interpersonal skills are a core ingredient in any Human Resource Development **(HRD)** effort. Ninety-six percent (96%) of the studies and 92% of the indices yield positive outcomes. Clearly, these helper effects hold across living, learning, and working outcomes.

2. **IPS training is the source of high levels of helper interpersonal functioning.**

   In all but ten instances, systematic **IPS** training was the source of helper interpersonal functioning. Thus, in 86% of the studies, **IPS** training was directly related to the effects of helping. That is to say, alone or in combination with other skills, **IPS** training is the significant source of effect in helping efforts.

(continued)

Summary Propositions *(concluded)*

3. **The effects of direct IPS training of recipients upon helpee outcomes are positive and significant.**

   The direct **IPS** training of recipients is a significant source of recipient outcome benefits. In 96% of the studies and 92% of the indices, the reported results were positive. Thus, alone or in combination with other skills, direct IPS training of recipients is a potential preferred model of treatment.

4. **Positive results are describable and predictable while negative results are statistical exceptions.**

   Ninety-six percent (96%) of the studies and 92% of the indices had positive outcomes. Thus, putting the issues of rater level of functioning and minimal level of helper functioning aside, it may be concluded that negative result studies and indices tend toward being statistical or random exceptions.

5. **Positive IPS outcomes are a consequence of systematic efforts while negative results are design exceptions.**

   Systematically derived results involve systematic design: systematic training design, systematic treatment design, systematic follow-up, and systematic environmental support. When present, these ingredients of systematic designs will yield systematic outcomes. When any one of these ingredients is absent, there is an increasing prospect for nonsignificant or even negative results. Thus, for example, without systematic training, variability in interpersonal functioning will be restricted and the relationships with various outcome indices become problematic.

Processing Skills

In this context, it is extremely important to emphasize IPS as processing skills, alone or in combination with other processing skills (see Table 6-1). In many of the studies, IPS are employed as the single intervention: the interveners are trained in IPS to intervene with the recipients, or the recipients are trained directly in IPS.

In other studies, IPS are employed in conjunction with other processing skills, such as problem-solving or cognitive-processing skills.

In summary, the most important issue is the critical nature of interpersonal skills. They serve to enable people to assume the frames of reference of others. They facilitate: the exploration of where others are in relation to a particular experience; the understanding of where others want or need to be; and the action behavior to get from where they are to where they want to be. In this regard, IPS are critical ingredients in the implementation of any programs involving human beings, whether individual, small-group, large-group, or community treatment or training. They may be used in conjunction with any other skills to accomplish any inter-vention goals involving humans in living, learning, and working performance.

Table 6-1.
A Summary Index of Percentages of Predominantly Positive Results of IPS Studies and Indices of Helpee Living, Learning, and Working Outcomes

OUTCOMES	HELPERS	HELPEES	OUTCOMES
LIVING			**LIVING**
Studies (N = 22)	91% Positive	92% Positive	Studies (N = 35)
Indices (N = 117)	83% Positive	83% Positive	Indices (N = 128)
LEARNING			**LEARNING**
Studies (N = 32)	97% Positive	100% Positive	Studies (N = 26)
Indices (N = 261)	92% Positive	99% Positive	Indices (N = 78)
WORKING			**WORKING**
Studies (N = 22)	100% Positive	100% Positive	Studies (N = 27)
Indices (N = 83)	96% Positive	98% Positive	Indices (N = 117)
SUBTOTAL			**SUBTOTAL**
Studies (N = 76)	96% Positive	96% Positive	Studies (N = 88)
Indices (N = 461)	92% Positive	92% Positive	Indices (N = 323)
GRAND TOTAL			
Studies (N = 164)	96% Positive		
Indices (N = 784)	92% Positive		

Applications and Transfers

The implications for parenting and helping, teaching and training, employing and working are profound. When helpers are trained to relate effectively to all levels within an organization—up and sideways as well as down—then they and their recipients are productive in achieving mutually beneficial goals. Furthermore, when the recipients are trained directly in relating effectively—up, down, and sideways—then they are productive in achieving their goals.

In this context, comprehensive intervention designs have been introduced in the areas of living, learning, and working skills.

Living

Intervention designs for living include the

- parenting skills training movement;
- lay counseling or "functional" professional movement;
- community-based mental health and medical movements;
- psychiatric rehabilitation movement;
- correctional counseling and youth diversion movements; and
- *"Possibilities Helper"* movement.

> For example, in the first comprehensive *"Possibilities Helper"* community-based project, Ralph Bierman and his associates demonstrated the living benefits of **IPS**-based, self-help, and community support programs throughout Canada. The project involved
>
> - community leaders;
> - professional helpers;
> - parents;
> - professional teachers; and
> - children.
>
> Basically, the project demonstrated that community citizens could be trained in **IPS**-based skills to, first, help themselves and, second, help others, including especially their children.

Learning

Intervention designs for learning include the

- "humanizing education" movement;
- "psychological education" movement;
- "lead teacher" movement;
- "relating model of discipline" movement;
- "learning-to-learn" movement;
- ***"Possibilities Teacher"*** movement.

For example, David Aspy, Flora Roebuck, and their associates conducted the first ***"Possibilities Teacher"*** projects as part of their **National Consortium for Humanizing Education.** They empowered tens of thousands of educators and children in **IPS** skills in more than 40 states and several foreign countries. This project involved

- principals;
- teachers; and
- learners.

They found that the learners of trained teachers thrived, while those of teachers who were not trained "plateaued" or deteriorated in scholastic and other kinds of performance.

Working

Intervention designs for working include the

- career development movement;
- career placement movement;
- "worker preparation" movement;
- **IPS**-based management movement;
- "Relating Up, Down, and Sideways" supervisory movement; and
- *"Possibilities Worker"* movement.

For example, in the first comprehensive demonstration of the *"Possibilities Worker,"* John Kelly and his associates in IBM's *"Office of the Future"* produced improved productivity benefits of **IPS**-based training with the following populations:

- Supervisors and managers
- Data managers
- Word processors

The project was so successful that the managers wanted to claim "ownership" due to their **"uniquely personalized management styles."**

The most comprehensive demonstration of the role of relating skills in the development of living, learning, and working skills was conducted by William Anthony, Mikal Cohen, and their associates in psychiatric rehabilitation. The researchers demonstrated positive outcomes with all elements of residential, educational, vocational, and community support systems as well as lobbying and legislative systems. Working in all 50 states and consulting throughout the world, they present their own relating-driven image of a futuristic mental health system:

A Vision for the Mental Health System for the Millennium

1. A mental health system in which people with psychiatric disabilities are viewed holistically as people with positive attributes, and treated accordingly

2. A mental health system committed to improving the residential, vocational, educational, and/or social status of each individual

3. A mental health system in which people with psychiatric disabilities play a major role in planning and implementing the new system

4. A mental health system that understands the importance of practitioners skilled in the technologies needed to achieve the processes and outcomes of psychiatric rehabilitation

5. A mental health system guided by the vision of recovery

(Anthony, Cohen, Farkas, and Gagne, 2001, p. 319)

Anthony himself summarized the implications of the effects of the relating skills orientation and the *"training as treatment"* approach to living, learning, and working skills application. Doing frequency tabulations of the word *skill* in the helping literature, he found few references prior to Carkhuff's 1974 keynote address to the American Personnel and Guidance Association. Subsequent to the address, the literature was replete with references to relating skills and living, learning, and working skills training as a **"preferred model of treatment."** The relating skills movement specifically and the life skills movement generically have changed the orientation to helping dramatically. Relating skills have helped make helping, teaching, and managing productive professions. Their influence remains profound in all areas of human endeavor.

In summary, **IPS** are critical human ingredients because they facilitate the accomplishment of human goals. **IPS** help people explore one anothers' frames of reference. **IPS** help people understand the objectives for the tasks at hand. Finally, **IPS** help people act on their shared objectives. In short, **IPS** facilitate the focusing of human efforts.

IPS help us to live more effectively with our families at home and to help more effectively our counselees in our counseling centers. **IPS** help us teach and learn more effectively in our schools and training centers. **IPS** help us work more effectively at our individual stations and in our organizations at work. In short, **IPS** facilitate our human productivity.

Overall, we stand about a 95 percent chance of accomplishing any human purposes when we have introduced **IPS** at high levels. Whether we train helpers or teachers or employers or their recipients in **IPS,** we accomplish our objectives far beyond the probabilities of chance. Conversely, when we do not introduce **IPS** at high levels, we stand a random chance of succeeding in any human endeavor. In conclusion, human productivity is in part a function of people's abilities to process interpersonally. Interpersonally skilled people, understanding each other accurately, can succeed at any reasonable human endeavor.

7

On Becoming Empathic

In the final analysis, human relations is about empathy— relating to help. Once again, the helper—parent, teacher, coach, minister, counselor, coworker, boss—is the **"more knowing person"** in the relationship. In turn, the **"less knowing person"** is the helpee—child, learner, parishioner, counselee, worker. We measure the effects of helping and human relations on the helpee's performance or behavior— **for better or for worse!**

Interpersonal Relating

When you think about it, there are two things that make us truly "human":

- The first is our ability to think.
- The second is our ability to relate.

Regarding our brainpower, each healthy human brain has approximately 100 billion neurons. Each of these neurons is more powerful than our most powerful **"state-of-the-art"** computers. Each of these neurons is capable of connecting simultaneously with 10,000 other neurons. Our brainpower is awesome.

Regarding our human relating skills, each healthy human also has the power for generating empathic responses to others. Empowered by our own neuronal processing, we have the potential for connecting with people in all kinds of circumstances. Happy or sad or angry, we can relate to the affect of their experience. Successful or failing or cheated, we can relate to the reason for their affect. Our relating skills are helping skills.

Indeed, when these two processes are integrated, we are at our most powerful in both relating and processing. When we relate interpersonally to process neuronally, our thinking is phenomenal. It is then that we can resolve the most difficult of human and social crises. We label this interpersonal process **"Get, Give, Merge"** or **GGM** (see Figure 7-1).

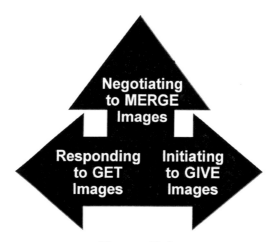

Figure 7-1.
Get, Give, Merge—Interpersonal Relating

Here is how it works:

> ### Get, Give, Merge
>
> • Responding to GET images.
> • Initiating to GIVE images.
> • Negotiating to MERGE images.

It is like a person seeking a position. He or she has a set of values. The position, itself, has a set of values that we label **"job requirements."** Together, applicant and job negotiate a merged image that maximizes meeting values and requirements at the highest levels.

There are variations of this interpersonal theme. One variation may be labeled reciprocal relating or interdependent relating. In these relationships, both parties are helpers, striving to generate new and better images of initiatives.

Parenting Crises

For example, it may be two parents relating interpersonally by mutual processing for mutual benefits:

Parent 1: I believe that the most important thing is that the kids experience freedom in their decision making.

Parent 2: You feel dedicated to free learning experiences.

Parent 1: And I know you are committed to their protection first and foremost.

Parent 2: I just get so anxious without knowing they're safe.

Parent 1: So someone has to take responsibility for their safety.

Parent 2: What are you saying, "You're confident that the kids can learn to be responsible for their own safety?"

Parent 1: I guess what I'm confident in is the basic principle of freedom—there is no freedom without responsibility.

Parent 2: I am confident in this principle—I guess we need a program for them to learn this.

In this manner—with sensitive responding, creative initiating, and balanced negotiating, **GGM** relating pays off in outcomes that define crises, generate solutions, and produce benefits:

GGM Family Outcomes

Merged opportunities for teenage "freedoms" (like malls and computers) with demonstrations of "responsibilities" (like safety precautions and remediation). These solutions help youth to understand that there is no freedom without responsibility: they meet the "freedom" values of youth and the "safety" requirements of adults at the highest levels.

Community Crises

We employed the same relating skills—**getting, giving, merging**—in community crises that we are already impacting:

Community Rep (CR1): The multinationals have abandoned the inner-city.

Consultant: It's terrifying to be without resources.

CR 2: It's even scarier to see what is happening to our kids.

Consultant: You're even more terrified of what they may become.

CR 2: If we abandon them, they may become criminals . . .

CR 1: Or worse yet, terrorists.

Consultant:	You're committed to doing everything you can to prevent that from happening?
CR 1:	Anything!
Consultant:	Would you consider making this an entrepreneurial community?
CR 2:	In other words, make our own money!
CR 1:	To learn how to generate our own wealth!
CR 2:	Is this possible?
Consultant:	You're excited to even consider it.
CR 1:	We'd be controlling our own destiny.
Consultant:	You're ecstatic about the possibilities.
CR 2:	We're eager to learn about this.

GGM Community Outcomes

Merged opportunities for full participation in generating wealth from womb to tomb in *"Entrepreneurial Communities"* instead of leaving inner-city youth unattended, vulnerable, and radicalized in *"Designs for Failure."* These communities will elevate the freedoms that yield the Three Principles of Civilization—Peace, Prosperity, Participation—to the point where they dwarf the outcomes of other communities.

These are truly **"Designs for Success"**!

Cultural Crises

We may project utilizing interpersonal relating skills in other kinds of conflicts, such as cultural or national:

- Getting another's images by responding empathically to their frames of reference
- Giving our own images that we can now personalize additively to incorporate the other's images
- Merging our images by maximizing each other's values and requirements

We can even project the benefits that may accrue from such interpersonal processing. Below is an illustration of some of the merged solutions that are already being proposed:

GGM Cultural Outcomes

Merged opportunities to participate in *"Enterprise Zones"* on the borders between Mexico and the United States (or between Palestine and Israel or Lebanon) as we seek economic rather than political or military answers. These solutions will generate productivity centers where per capita Gross Domestic Product growth exceeds the most prosperous metro center of the United States.

In summary, these are not the fantasies of our imagination or the compromises of political realities. These are the legitimate creative merged initiatives of our generation. We do not have to be **"trapped"** by the probabilities of a world designed before us. We can relate to each other. We can help each other.

As may be noted, time is telescoped as each new age culminates the contributions of the previous age:

- **The Agricultural Age** multiplied the benefits of **hunter-gathering** many times over.
- **The Industrial Age** multiplied the benefits of **The Agriculture Age** more than a hundred-fold.
- Now as **The Information Age** transitions into **The Ideation Age,** it will multiply the benefits of **The Industrial Age** exponentially.

In short, new possibilities actualize old probabilities.

In transition, there are the two things that make this enormous productivity possible: **human relating** and **human processing.** Together, they converge on the third characteristic of humanity: **change.** To be sure, change is the characteristic that best defines our humanity. By being introduced to helping and human relating, we are on our way to becoming truly human.

We may add:

> **"You feel empowered by this knowledge because you can now respond to all kinds of situations."**

All you have to do is begin by relating to the other person's experience, **"You . . ."**

You are now accountable!

Everything matters!

8

The Heart
of Empathy

Empathy is the ultimate expression of freedom for both helper and helpee. By responding empathically to another's experience, the helper freely opens his or her own ego boundaries to incorporate those of another. Similarly, by opening up to another's empathic understanding, the helpee increases the degrees of freedom of his or her ego boundaries.

Regarding empathic relating skills, each healthy human has the brainpower for generating accurately empathic responses to others. Helpers or helpees, we all have the potential for connecting with people in all kinds of circumstances. Happy or sad or angry, we can relate to the affect of their experiences. Successful or failing or cheated, we can relate to the meaning or the reason for their affect.

Indeed, we may view the relating process as empowering the helpees to become helpers. In a very real sense, the helpees share their experiences with helpers in order to learn to relate empathically with their own experiences. This is the most liberating of all human interactions.

To be sure, we are most free and powerful when we view the relationship as sharing with each other. When we relate empathically to process ideationally, our interpersonal thinking is phenomenal. It is then that we free ourselves to negotiate reactively resolutions to the most difficult of human crises and generate proactively solutions to the most elevated of social missions.

By sharing images, we free ourselves to generate new images that maximize meeting the values and requirements involved. Moreover, by relating images, empathy entrusts all of us to defining our own destinies.

There is a still more profound level of freedom available to us in **"Virtual Processing."** Here, with the conquering of the substance of the phenomena involved, we can become **"one"** with the phenomena. Like the great artists and scientists, we can process interdependently with the phenomena, generating creative **"breakthroughs"** that the world has never before seen.

In this regard, empathy serves **"virtual processor"** as well as phenomena.

Freedom! *"**You have to give it up to get it!**"*

In the final analysis, then, empathy is more than responding—however accurately—to another person's experience. For some, empathy is encoded in human nature by our **DNA:** it is simply a matter of releasing our instincts to relate.

For others, empathy is shaped by tens of thousands of years of **"sociogenetic encoding"** that we call **"civilization":** relating to others the way we want them to relate to us.

For many, empathy is reverentially entrusted to us by God: we relate on earth to prepare for our afterlife in heaven.

But, "heavy" as they are, empathy is more than all these sources. Empathy is a sacred trust. It emphasizes entering inviolable **"space"**—the personal space of another human. With earned **"permission,"** this is indeed a heavy trust. Without permission—as with a reluctant helpee—it is a profound burden.

The trust is sacred because we ourselves must be **"sanctified":** pure in our intentions, pure in our understanding. This trust is not to be abused! The consequences of abuse are profound for trustor and trustee.

The trust is sacred because we must be **"wise":** wise in our knowledge of systems, wise in our commitment to solutions.

Finally, the trust is sacred because we must be **"special"**: special because we will leave others better than we found them, special because we ourselves will grow in these relationships.

All of these experiences converge to generate the sacredness or purity of empathy.

The Sacred Feeling

- With empathy, we experience special growth with others. Some call it "Mutual Relating for Mutual Growth." We label it "Love."

- With empathy, we introduce the principle of "reciprocity." Some call it "Reciprocal Relating" whereby people relate empathically to each other. We label it "Civilization."

- With empathy, we generate all things that were promised to us by our ancestors' evolution and our own individual development. No problem is above resolution. No growth is beyond achievement. Some call it "Helping." We label it "The Heart of Empathy."

In transition, empathy is **"The Sacred Feeling"** that makes us truly **"human"**—no longer **"humankind."** We define ourselves as human by how we empathize with the humanity in other people.

Most powerful of all, empathy is the source of **"human optimism."** We respond to past and present only to generate an increasingly accurate vision of our future.

We define ourselves as human by our profound belief in change—our personal change, the other's change, our world's change. We invest ourselves in empathic relating as an expression of our optimism in our ever-changing human identities:

I Am Change

If they are young who think
That they can change the world,
I am a newborn infant
I am change unfurled.
You can chalk me on the blackboards
Or scratch me in the sand.
You can shout me in the chorus
That builds throughout the land.

You can see me in the eyes of children
And hear me in their song.
You can taste my sweet breath in the wind
And feel me being born.

You can find me in the skills you learn—
You can use my eyes to see.
For when they teach you what is known,
You'll discover what can be.
You can join me in the nation's womb
As we fashion our freedom.
For I am change and change alone
Can forge a human being.

You can see me in the eyes of children
And hear me in their song.
You can taste my sweet breath in the wind
And feel me being born.

Appendix

Process and Outcome Research

The research on Human Relating began with the break-through insight of the **"interchangeability of responding"**:

> **Could one person (the helper) have communi-cated what the other person (the helpee) had communicated in terms of the feeling and meaning and the content of the expression?**

The interchangeable response enabled us to assess the effectiveness of all helping and human relationships.

What we discovered was astounding. Some helpers—parents, teachers, counselors, managers—never made an interchangeable response—never, ever! How, then, could they help others achieve their objectives? Other helpers—fewer than 5 of 100—would periodically check back with their helpees by making interchangeable responses.

The outcomes followed the processes. The helpees of helpers who made interchangeable responses improved on a whole variety of indices. The helpees of the **"helpers"** who did not make interchangeable responses stayed the same or even declined on a variety of indices.

Again: **all learning begins with the learner's frame of reference.**

The ingredients of interpersonal relating evolved as we conducted further research in response to a number of challenges to the helping profession. In the process, we became among the first to find that helping may be *"for better or for worse,"* that is, facilitative or retarding—a finding with significant implications for parents, teachers, counselors, therapists, managers, and the like. Moreover, we also discovered that we could account for the facilitative or retarding effects by the helpers' levels of functioning on certain scaled dimensions, such as empathic relating or responding.

It is worthwhile to view the models of relating that evolved through living, learning, and working applications associated with this research.

The Relating Models

The main effect of empathic relating on the part of the helper was to facilitate exploration of experience on the part of the helpee. With that, we had our first model for helping: *helper responding facilitates the helpee's experiential exploring of problems* (see Figure A-1).

Helper Skills: **Responding**

↓

Helpees'
Experience: **EXPLORING**

Figure A-1.
Early Model for Helping

Eclectically drawing upon all theoretical orientations, we explored many scaled dimensions and then factor-analyzed them. We discovered that these dimensions "loaded" upon two discrete interpersonal factors:

- Responding that emphasized empathy, respect, and warmth in relating to other people's frames of reference

- Initiating that emphasized genuineness, concreteness, and self-disclosure of the helper's own experiences

With these results, we had a basic model for helping (see Figure A-2):

- Responding facilitates exploring.
- Initiating stimulates acting.

The helpees could now act upon their explorations of experience.

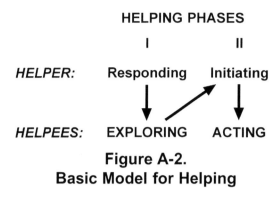

Figure A-2.
Basic Model for Helping

Further requirements of the interpersonal dimensions yielded a transitional dimension between responding and initiating, based on the personalizing factor:

Personalizing that emphasized immediacy of experiencing, confrontation, and internalizing, especially as it relates to responsibility for one's actions

With that, the researchers had a transitional model for helping (see Figure A-3):

Personalizing facilitates understanding.

The helpees could now act based upon their self-understanding.

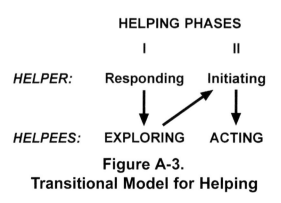

Figure A-3.
Transitional Model for Helping

The comprehensive model was not completed until other factors were analyzed and incorporated. Foremost among these factors was attending:

Attending that emphasizes paying attention to others by attending physically, observing their appearance and behavior, and listening to their expressions of their experience

With that, the researchers had a comprehensive model for engaging or involving others in the helping process (see Figure A-4):

> - Attending facilitates involving.
> - Responding facilitates exploring.
> - Personalizing facilitates understanding.
> - Initiating facilitates acting.

The helpers could now engage the helpees in a comprehensive helping process.

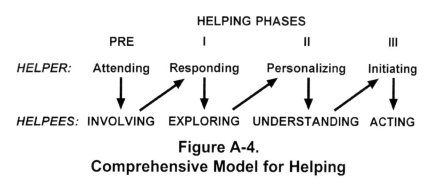

Figure A-4.
Comprehensive Model for Helping

Finally, feedback is recycled for continuous and improved processing (see Figure A-5):

- More intensive involving
- More extensive exploring
- More accurate understanding
- More effective acting

Both helpees and helpers now had a comprehensive model for continuous processing of increasingly productive responses.

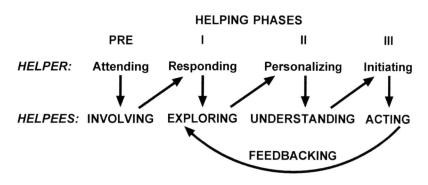

Figure A-5.
Continuous Processing Model for Helping

Learning

With educational applications and analyses, the helping model was expanded to incorporate teaching skills (see Figure A-6). As we may see:

> • Content development plus attending facilitates involving.
>
> • Diagnosing plus responding facilitates exploring.
>
> • Learning objectives plus personalizing facilitates understanding.
>
> • Individualizing learning programs plus initiating facilitates acting.

Again, feedback is recycled to facilitate a more productive teaching-learning process. Both teachers and learners could now implement a comprehensive model for learning.

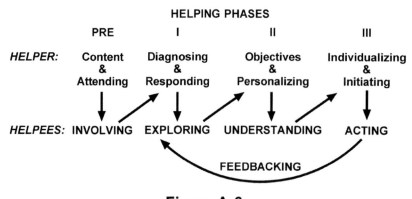

Figure A-6.
Comprehensive Model for Teaching

Working

With working applications and analyses, the helping/teaching model was expanded to incorporate working and thinking skills (see Figure A-7). As we may see:

- Goaling plus content and attending facilitate involving.
- Expanding plus diagnosing and responding facilitate exploring.
- Narrowing plus objectives and personalizing facilitate understanding.
- Programming plus individualizing and initiating facilitate acting.

Once again, feedback is recycled to facilitate the most productive working-thinking process. Managers and supervisors and workers now had a comprehensive model for working and thinking on the job.

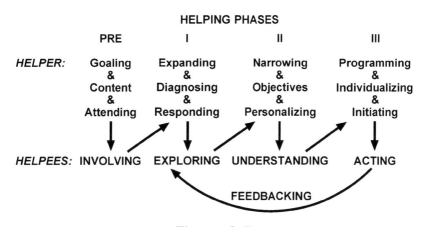

Figure A-7.
Comprehensive Model for Working and Thinking

With our associates, we went on to make demonstrations of the effects of relating interventions in all areas of human experience: parenting, education, counseling, psychotherapy, and business/industry management and supervision.

Moreover, we made demonstrations of the effects of direct relating-skills training upon helpees in all areas of human experience: children, learners, counselees, patients, employees, and supervisees. In doing so, they introduced their principle of **"training as treatment"** or **"psychological education"** as a preferred model of treatment. Here is what the research yielded.

Process and Outcome

The effects of interpersonal-skills, or **IPS,** dimensions were summarized by the researchers in a review of 164 studies of more than 160,000 people. In this review, we find several sets of summary propositions drawn from these results as well as their processing-skills implications (Carkhuff, 1983).

Summary Propositions

1. **The effects of helper interpersonal functioning upon recipient outcomes are positive and significant.**

   A summary of the effects of helpers upon helpee outcome indices suggests that interpersonal skills are a core ingredient in any Human Resource Development **(HRD)** effort. Ninety-six percent (96%) of the studies and 92% of the indices yield positive outcomes. Clearly, these helper effects hold across living, learning, and working outcomes.

2. **IPS training is the source of high levels of helper interpersonal functioning.**

   In all but ten instances, systematic **IPS** training was the source of helper interpersonal functioning. Thus, in 86% of the studies, **IPS** training was directly related to the effects of helping. That is to say, alone or in combination with other skills, **IPS** training is the significant source of effect in helping efforts.

(continued)

Summary Propositions *(concluded)*

3. **The effects of direct IPS training of recipients upon helpee outcomes are positive and significant.**

   The direct **IPS** training of recipients is a significant source of recipient outcome benefits. In 96% of the studies and 92% of the indices, the reported results were positive. Thus, alone or in combination with other skills, direct IPS training of recipients is a potential preferred model of treatment.

4. **Positive results are describable and predictable while negative results are statistical exceptions.**

   Ninety-six percent (96%) of the studies and 92% of the indices had positive outcomes. Thus, putting the issues of rater level of functioning and minimal level of helper functioning aside, it may be concluded that negative result studies and indices tend toward being statistical or random exceptions.

5. **Positive IPS outcomes are a consequence of systematic efforts while negative results are design exceptions.**

   Systematically derived results involve systematic design: systematic training design, systematic treatment design, systematic follow-up, and systematic environmental support. When present, these ingredients of systematic designs will yield systematic outcomes. When any one of these ingredients is absent, there is an increasing prospect for nonsignificant or even negative results. Thus, for example, without systematic training, variability in interpersonal functioning will be restricted and the relationships with various outcome indices become problematic.

Processing Skills

In this context, it is extremely important to emphasize IPS as processing skills, alone or in combination with other processing skills (see Table A-1). In many of the studies, IPS are employed as the single intervention: the interveners are trained in IPS to intervene with the recipients, or the recipients are trained directly in IPS.

In other studies, IPS are employed in conjunction with other processing skills, such as problem-solving or cognitive-processing skills.

In summary, the most important issue is the critical nature of interpersonal skills. They serve to enable people to assume the frames of reference of others. They facilitate: the exploration of where others are in relation to a particular experience; the understanding of where others want or need to be; and the action behavior to get from where they are to where they want to be. In this regard, IPS are critical ingredients in the implementation of any programs involving human beings, whether individual, small-group, large-group, or community treatment or training. They may be used in conjunction with any other skills to accomplish any intervention goals involving humans in living, learning, and working performance (Carkhuff, 1983, pp. 82–91).

Table A-1.
A Summary Index of Percentages of Predominantly Positive Results of IPS Studies and Indices of Helpee Living, Learning, and Working Outcomes

OUTCOMES	HELPERS	HELPEES	OUTCOMES
LIVING			**LIVING**
Studies (N = 22)	91% Positive	92% Positive	Studies (N = 35)
Indices (N = 117)	83% Positive	83% Positive	Indices (N = 128)
LEARNING			**LEARNING**
Studies (N = 32)	97% Positive	100% Positive	Studies (N = 26)
Indices (N = 261)	92% Positive	99% Positive	Indices (N = 78)
WORKING			**WORKING**
Studies (N = 22)	100% Positive	100% Positive	Studies (N = 27)
Indices (N = 83)	96% Positive	98% Positive	Indices (N = 117)
SUBTOTAL			**SUBTOTAL**
Studies (N = 76)	96% Positive	96% Positive	Studies (N = 88)
Indices (N = 461)	92% Positive	92% Positive	Indices (N = 323)
GRAND TOTAL			
Studies (N = 164)	**96% Positive**		
Indices (N = 784)	**92% Positive**		

Applications and Transfers

The implications for parenting and helping, teaching and training, employing and working are profound. When helpers are trained to relate effectively to all levels within an organization—up and sideways as well as down—then they and their recipients are productive in achieving mutually beneficial goals. Furthermore, when the recipients are trained directly in relating effectively—up, down, and sideways—then they are productive in achieving their goals.

In this context, comprehensive intervention designs have been introduced in the areas of living, learning, and working skills.

Living

Intervention designs for living include the

- parenting skills training movement;
- lay counseling or "functional" professional movement;
- community-based mental health and medical movements;
- psychiatric rehabilitation movement;
- correctional counseling and youth diversion movements; and
- *"Possibilities Helper"* movement.

For example, in the first comprehensive *"Possibilities Helper"* community-based project, Ralph Bierman and his associates demonstrated the living benefits of **IPS**-based, self-help, and community support programs throughout Canada. The project involved

- community leaders;
- professional helpers;
- parents;
- professional teachers; and
- children.

Basically, the project demonstrated that community citizens could be trained in **IPS**-based skills to, first, help themselves and, second, help others, including especially their children.

Learning

Intervention designs for learning include the

- "humanizing education" movement;
- "psychological education" movement;
- "lead teacher" movement;
- "relating model of discipline" movement;
- "learning-to-learn" movement;
- ***"Possibilities Teacher"*** movement.

For example, David Aspy, Flora Roebuck, and associates conducted the first ***"Possibilities Teacher"*** projects as part of their **National Consortium for Humanizing Education.** They empowered tens of thousands of educators and children in **IPS** skills in more than 40 states and several foreign countries. This project involved

- principals;
- teachers; and
- learners.

They found that the learners of trained teachers thrived, while those of teachers who were not trained "plateaued" or deteriorated in scholastic and other kinds of performance.

Working

Intervention designs for working include the

- career development movement;
- career placement movement;
- "worker preparation" movement;
- **IPS**-based management movement;
- "Relating Up, Down, and Sideways" supervisory movement; and
- *"Possibilities Worker"* movement.

For example, in the first comprehensive demonstration of the *"Possibilities Worker,"* John Kelly and his associates in IBM's *"Office of the Future"* produced improved productivity benefits of **IPS**-based training with the following populations:

- Supervisors and managers
- Data managers
- Word processors

The project was so successful that the managers wanted to claim "ownership" due to their **"uniquely personalized management styles."**

The most comprehensive demonstration of the role of relating skills in the development of living, learning, and working skills was conducted by William Anthony, Mikal Cohen, and their associates in psychiatric rehabilitation. The researchers demonstrated positive outcomes with all elements of residential, educational, vocational, and community support systems as well as lobbying and legislative systems. Working in all 50 states and consulting throughout the world, they present their own relating-driven image of a futuristic mental health system:

A Vision for the Mental Health System for the Millennium

1. A mental health system in which people with psychiatric disabilities are viewed holistically as people with positive attributes, and treated accordingly

2. A mental health system committed to improving the residential, vocational, educational, and/or social status of each individual

3. A mental health system in which people with psychiatric disabilities play a major role in planning and implementing the new system

4. A mental health system that understands the importance of practitioners skilled in the technologies needed to achieve the processes and outcomes of psychiatric rehabilitation

5. A mental health system guided by the vision of recovery

(Anthony, Cohen, Farkas, and Gagne, 2001, p. 319)

Anthony himself summarized the implications of the effects of the relating skills orientation and the *"training as treatment"* approach to living, learning, and working skills application. Doing frequency tabulations of the word *skill* in the helping literature, he found few references prior to Carkhuff's 1974 keynote address to the American Personnel and Guidance Association. Subsequent to the address, the literature was replete with references to relating skills and living, learning, and working skills training as a **"preferred model of treatment."** The relating skills movement specifically and the life skills movement generically have changed the orientation to helping dramatically. Relating skills have helped make helping, teaching, and managing productive professions. Their influence remains profound in all areas of human endeavor.

In summary, **IPS** are critical human ingredients because they facilitate the accomplishment of human goals. **IPS** help people explore one anothers' frames of reference. **IPS** help people understand the objectives for the tasks at hand. Finally, **IPS** help people act on their shared objectives. In short, **IPS** facilitate the focusing of human efforts.

IPS help us to live more effectively with our families at home and to help more effectively our counselees in our counseling centers. **IPS** help us teach and learn more effectively in our schools and training centers. **IPS** help us work more effectively at our individual stations and in our organizations at work. In short, **IPS** facilitate our human productivity.

Overall, we stand about a 95 percent chance of accomplishing any human purposes when we have introduced **IPS** at high levels. Whether we train helpers or teachers or employers or their recipients in **IPS,** we accomplish our objectives far beyond the probabilities of chance. Conversely, when we do not introduce **IPS** at high levels, we stand a random chance of succeeding in any human endeavor. In conclusion, human productivity is in part a function of people's abilities to process interpersonally. Interpersonally skilled people, understanding each other accurately, can succeed at any reasonable human endeavor.

References

Anthony, W. A. *The Principles of Psychiatric Rehabilitation.* Baltimore, MD: University Park Press, 1979.

Anthony, W. A., Cohen, M., Farkas, M., and Gagne, C. *Psychiatric Rehabilitation.* Boston, MA: Center for Psychiatric Rehabilitation, 2001.

Aspy, D. N., and Roebuck, F. N. *Kids Don't Learn from People They Don't Like.* Amherst, MA: HRD Press, 1978.

Berenson, B. G., and Cannon, J. R. *The Science of Freedom.* McLean, VA: American Nobel Prize, 2007.

Berenson, B. G., and Carkhuff, R. R. *Sources of Gain in Counseling and Psychotherapy.* Amherst, MA: HRD Press, 1967.

Berenson, B. G., and Carkhuff, R. R. *The Possibilities Mind.* Amherst, MA: HRD Press, 2001.

Berenson, B. G., and Mitchell, K. M. *Confrontation.* Amherst, MA: HRD Press, 1974.

Bierman, R. *Toward Meeting Fundamental Human Service Needs.* Guelph, Ontario: Human Service Community, Inc., 1976.

Carkhuff, R. R. *Helping and Human Relations. Volume I.* Selection and Training. New York: Holt, Rinehart & Winston, 1969.

Carkhuff, R. R. *Helping and Human Relations. Volume II.* Practice and Research. New York: Holt, Rinehart & Winston, 1969.

Carkhuff, R. R. *Human Possibilities.* Amherst, MA: HRD Press, 2000.

Carkhuff, R. R. *IPS—Interpersonal Skills and Human Productivity.* Amherst, MA: HRD Press, 1983.

Carkhuff, R. R. *The Age of Ideation.* McLean, VA: American Nobel Prize, 2007.

Carkhuff, R. R. *The Art of Helping. 8th Edition.* Amherst, MA: HRD Press, 1972, 2000.

Carkhuff, R. R. *The Development of Human Resources.* New York: Holt, Rinehart & Winston, 1971.

Carkhuff, R. R., and Benoit, D. *The New 3Rs.* Amherst, MA: HRD Press, 2008.

Carkhuff, R. R., and Berenson, B. G. *Beyond Counseling and Therapy.* New York: Holt, Rinehart & Winston, 1967.

Carkhuff, R. R., and Berenson, B. G. *Teaching as Treatment.* Amherst, MA: HRD Press, 1976.

Carkhuff, R. R., and Berenson, B. G. *The New Science of Possibilities, Volumes I and II.* Amherst, MA: HRD Press, 2000.

Carkhuff, R. R., and Berenson, B. G. *The Possibilities Leader.* Amherst, MA: HRD Press, 2000.

Carkhuff, R. R., and Berenson, B. G. *The Possibilities Organization.* Amherst, MA: HRD Press, 2000.

Friel, T. W. *Educational and Career Exploration System.* New York: IBM, Inc., 1972.

Kelly, J. T. *The Effects of IPS Training Upon Word Processing Output in the Office of the Future.* New York: IBM, Inc., 1983.

Truax, C. B., and Carkhuff, R. R. *Toward Effective Counseling and Psychotherapy.* Chicago: Aldine, 1967.